CABBAGES FOR THE KING

ADRIAN PLASS

Cabbages for the King

Illustrated by Ben Ecclestone

Fount
An Imprint of HarperCollinsPublishers

Fount Paperbacks is an Imprint of
HarperCollins*Religious*
Part of HarperCollins*Publishers*
77–85 Fulham Palace Road,
Hammersmith, London W6 8JB

First published in Great Britain
in 1993 by Fount Paperbacks

1 3 5 7 9 10 8 6 4 2

Copyright in the text © 1993 Adrian Plass
Copyright in the illustrations © 1993 Ben Ecclestone

Adrian Plass and Ben Ecclestone assert the moral right to
be identified as the author and illustrator of this work

A catalogue record for this book
is available from the British Library

ISBN 0 00 627668 7

Printed and bound in Great Britain by
HarperCollinsManufacturing Glasgow

CONTENTS

TO THE READER

Why is this book called *Cabbages for the King*?

The simple answer is that, on one very important level, being a Christian who happens to speak and write about his faith is much the same as being a Christian who happens to run a greengrocer's shop.

The conscientious greengrocer buys and sells the best produce he can get, in as pleasant a manner as possible, at a price that is appropriate to the resources of his customers and the needs of his own family. He does not (unless he is a a greengrocer with private means) have the option of not coming in to work on those mornings when he feels spiritually barren. The public need their cabbages, and an unsanctified cabbage tastes much the same as a sanctified one. The believing greengrocer is an ordinary man trying to live up to his high calling. Day by day he does his best to provide people with what they need, and asks God to protect his customers and himself from his own shortcomings.

So do I.

When the greengrocer and I arrive in heaven together, we shall be equal in the eyes of God, except that I (hopefully) will be known by my fruit, whereas he will be known by his fruit *and* veg.

This book is a collection of the jokes, stories, sketches and verse that I, and more recently my wife and I, have flung at people from platforms all over the country. Most of them are humorous (or are supposed to be), a few are sad or serious, and the rest are beyond definition.

Such as they are, they are what I do for God – cabbages for the King. I hope you enjoy them.

TELLING THE TRUTH

Truth enters the mind so easily that when we hear it for the first time it seems as if we were simply recalling it to memory.

BERNARD DE FONTENELLE 1768

Truths and roses have thorns about them.

H. G. BOHN – Handbook of proverbs 1855

Truth stretches but does not break.

Spanish proverb

Telling the Truth

How do you start a book? I never know how to start anything. Quite often, when I stand up to speak in churches or halls or theatres, I haven't the faintest idea what I'm going to say. This doesn't matter so much nowadays because I don't get as frightened as I used to, but in the early days my nervous system took a terrible pounding every time.

Recently, after arriving at a venue by the skin of my teeth, I began with the following words:

"I just want to thank my lucky stars that . . ."

I stopped as I realized that among those present there would almost certainly be a number who were astrologically challenged. Most people laughed when I changed my remark to: "I just want to thank the Lord that . . .", but some did not.

Oh, dear!

Apart from the fact that I'm constitutionally incapable of putting together a logical sequence of ideas or points and then sticking to it (my tangential tendencies do occasionally cause a little conflict when my wife and I are working together), this inability to find a starting place is probably something to do with identity. I don't seem to fit into any of the traditional categories of Christian speaker. I'm not a preacher, I'm certainly not a Bible teacher and it's a long time since I've been allowed to just entertain. What I do have is a determination to live, privately and publicly, with the gap between what I am and what I think I ought to be. I don't mean that I won't change for the better – God is always making that possible in our lives – but I refuse to pretend that my virtue or spirituality is cubed just because I'm standing on a platform.

We shall never match our message, so I think it is probably more useful to tell the truth. Enthusiasm and optimism are no substitutes for reality.

I remember working with an evangelist in the Midlands once. It was an evening meeting and the large hall in which we were operating was about half full. I went on stage first and spoke for fifteen minutes or so, then he came on to do the main talk. Now, for those who don't know, evangelists are a fine body of men, but they find it very difficult to believe that anyone can absorb or understand any piece of information unless it has been repeated about thirty-nine times. This fellow was no exception. When, in retrospect, I add this tendency to the aforementioned inability to separate personal and divine truth, what followed was not really very surprising. I can't remember the exact wording of my colleague's address, but here is an approximation of one whole chunk of what he said.

"I don't worry, because I belong to God. I belong to God, so I don't have to worry. Why don't I worry? Well, it's because I belong to God. Who do I belong to? It's God, of course, and because of that I don't have to worry. Worry? Me? I don't! Why should I when I belong to God? You see, belonging to God means the end of worry, and that's something I don't do now that I belong to God . . ."

Several permutations later the evangelist concluded his talk, left the stage, and came into the wings where I was waiting. His whispered words took my breath away.

"I'm really worried," he said hoarsely, "I don't think I got through to them at all."

I was shocked. I hadn't been in the crinkly-eyed business for very long and I still believed that – by and large – Christian speakers were honest about themselves.

"Hold on a minute," I replied, "you just told all those

people out there that you don't worry because you belong to God. What about that?"

"Ah, well," he said, "I was preaching then."

It's so easy to get carried away like that. I've done it myself. But, balanced against experiences like the one I've just mentioned, which might make one very cynical, are some overwhelming truths.

First, nothing has changed. The message always was going to be greater than we are. John the Baptist, languishing in Herod's prison, wanted to know if Jesus really was "the one". Only a short time ago, filled with the Holy Spirit, he had confidently identified the Messiah in front of crowds of people at the river bank. Now, crouched in the confining darkness, faced with his own limitations, he felt wretchedly uncertain.

God uses inadequate people. He has to. They're the only sort available to choose from. He is committed to the risk of entrusting his earthly image to idiots like you, me, and my evangelist friend, people who will fail and make mistakes from time to time.

Secondly, there are many wonderful and authentically God-inspired events and miracles happening in the Church nowadays. Sadly human nature is such that many people notice absurdity, failure and vain empire-building much more readily than the things of God. You, me and the evangelist had better work even harder to keep silliness to a minimum.

There's an illustration often used in philosophical discussions on the subject of creativity. It concerns a cynic who rips apart a beautiful picture.

"I told you so!" he exclaims triumphantly. "There is no picture here. It's just a collection of wood, canvas, nails and pigment. You're all deceiving yourselves!"

He's wrong, of course. There *is* a picture, and it's so much more than the sum of its component parts.

The Church, the body of Christ, is exactly the same. Any

cynic could examine my life, or the strange antics of my Christian brothers and sisters, and say, "There's nothing here – there's just Adrian Plass and these other ridiculous bits and pieces. There *is* no Church. There is no body of Christ. There is no God!"

How sadly wrong he would be. The bride, the body, the face and hands of God on earth, quickened by the Holy Spirit, and led by the mind and will of Jesus himself must be a beautiful picture when it's viewed from Heaven. God loves to look at this work of art, and I'm so glad he's painted me into one small corner.

He has given me permission to be honest about him *and* myself, and that's what I shall go on doing.

It seems very fitting that this first selection of pieces should be concerned with Truth, because Truth is the wholesaler from whom most of my "cabbages" are obtained.

Am I the Only One?

One of my greatest fears as a young Christian was that, by some impossible means, the person I really was inside would be revealed to all the other people in my church. What would they say and think when they saw the swamp that my mind often became? How would they cope with the knowledge that I stopped believing in God altogether sometimes, or that my daily "quiet time" was not daily at all, but weekly, or fortnightly, or monthly, or even less frequent than that? Could they accommodate a mess?

Nowadays I'm much less bothered about people knowing what I'm really like, but I shall always experience a slight sense of loneliness about being the only person, in terms of personality and outlook, who is my unique shape. I will never find another me to compare notes with (what a blessed relief for the rest of the world!), but, unique as each of us is, we do all have an awful lot in common. In fact, it can be breathtakingly liberating to discover that you are *not* "the only one".

Am I the Only One?

Am I the only one
Who follows God,
Nottingham Forest,
Neighbours
And his own inclinations – usually in reverse order?
I do hope not.

Am I the only one
Who likes Norman Wisdom films,

Bat out of Hell,
Little House on the Prairie,
and *Silence of the Lambs?*
Probably.

Am I the only one
Who hasn't learned to drive,
Probably never will,
Doesn't want to,
And might well murder the next person who asks why not?
Maybe.

Am I the only one
Who checks his sitting-room carpet for big bits before
    hoovering it
Then afterwards finds the suction pipe blocked with dead
    dogs,
Half bricks, rolls of prairie wire, nests of tiddly winks,
Most of the *Sunday Times* and six pound fifty in small
    change?
I doubt it.

Am I the only one
Who talks to himself loudly when he's alone
Then suddenly realizes he isn't,
Feels like a loony,
And tries to make it sound like a song?
Surely not.

Am I the only one
Who hates all criticism,
Especially the constructive sort,
Because that usually means
I have to do something about it?
I don't think so.

Am I the only one
Who likes to have his cake,
Eat it,
Sick it up,
Then feel sorry for himself?
Possibly.

Am I the only one
Who loves and needs love,
And fails and falls and cries,
And takes the hand of anyone whose turn it is to be strong,
Whose turn it is to be Jesus for me?
Am I the only one?

Jenny

I wish that, as a Church, we were more willing to share our
shadows as well as our shining. What a shadowy event the
crucifixion must have been – and what a shining outcome.

People can accept the *whole* story, however grainy and
granular it may seem, much more readily than a carefully
edited one.

Not long after Jenny Larcombe was miraculously healed
(only those who did not know her before and after her
healing could doubt that) the sister of a very close friend of
ours committed suicide after years of depressive illness. She
happened to be called Jenny too. She was a follower of
Jesus, struggling against all the odds to remain stable
enough to lead a normal life. She tried very hard, but in the
end she failed, just as those who are suffering from severe
physical illnesses quite often fail to recover. I would like
the Church to own *both* of these Jennys, because they both
belong to Jesus, equal citizens in the Kingdom of God.

Of course the mystery remains, but it is a mystery with a
heart.

Jenny

Our father who art in heaven,
Jenny walked in front of a train last night,
Hallowed be thy name, thy kingdom come,
She was only thirty-seven,
Thy will be done on earth, as it is in heaven,
You knew what she was going to do, didn't you, Lord?
Give us this day our daily bread,
She had no hope left,

God's Bridge

And forgive us our trespasses as we forgive those who
   trespass against us.
Jenny is forgiven, isn't she?
Lead us not into temptation,
Lots of us are on the edge of darkness,
And deliver us from evil,
The only strength we have is yours,
For thine is the Kingdom,
And she's living there now,
The power and the glory,
She's yours, Lord,
For ever and ever,
Jenny,
Amen.

Diet

It is impossible to over-emphasize the connection between physical well-being and spiritual peace. I'm not, of course, suggesting that one depends upon the other, because many wonderful people have demonstrated great serenity of spirit in the midst of suffering. I'm simply pointing out that a number of people I know (including myself) have discovered that tiredness, too much alcohol, and over-eating, to name but three little items, have the effect of dulling one's awareness of spiritual things.

I know someone who felt far from God for years, and made no progress at all until she went on a strict diet and began to like herself again. This is not a moral statement that I'm making, although (forgive me) it becomes one as soon as we see the truth of it, but a matter of practical living.

I crouch miserably in my hovel of hypocrisy as I write these words. I get very tired. I do enjoy a drink. I expand and contract like a bull-frog's throat.

Read the words that follow, have mercy on me, and I'll have mercy on you.

Diet

expansion was not good business for my body
then I replaced the four sugars in my tea
with sweeteners no after taste eh funny
fat out fibre shovelled in or through
got a shade depressed a little blue
a friend told me alcohol inflates
gave up claret very nearly died
no more boozing nothing fried
full of tuna fish and dates
planned to cheat but then
a miracle I saw my feet
like other better men
fresh air was sweet
and nature smiled
I ran and leapt
soundly   slept
happy   child
so   serene
so   lean
a   bit
fit
I
ate
a   bit
a   treat
or   trophy
had a steak
a   titchy cake
a   glass of port
a   prize I thought
for   dieting so well
oh I smiled as I fell
suddenly I wanted chops
wild eyed I hit the shops
syrup jams and lemon cheese
spring into my trolley please
soggy doughnuts filled with jam
come and make me sticky here I am
chocolate fancy and chocolate plain
welcome to the orbit of my face again
crinkly crunkly crunchy fat fried chips
how I do desire to squelch you in my lips
expansion was not good business for my body

Christmas

Here's the scenario.

The angel Pongo appears in your sitting room at midnight on Christmas Eve, and makes the following speech,

"Greetings, highly favoured one. Behold, the Lord has appointed me to bring you news of great joy. Namely, that thou hast built up such a multitude of Brownie points with thy constant do-goodings and such, that he wisheth to offer thee anything that thy heart desireth, even unto a brand new motor or a holiday in the Algarve with bath and all facilities, or, if thou opteth for such, something more useful but less material, if thou getteth my drift."

"What, you mean like the knowledge that I am following faithfully in the steps of my beloved master?"

"Well, yes, that sort of thing. Most of them tendeth to go for a Porsche, actually, but what you said would go down like a dose of salts in terms of thy future standing with the boss, him being exceedingly big on humility and the like. Suit thyself, but bear in mind that the boss valueth the truth above silver and gold. If thou fancieth a Porsche but asketh for a cold bath and septic boils he will bloweth his stack – take mine word for it."

So, what would you choose if Pongo asked you?

What would *I* choose?

Whatever I wanted, eh?

Well, it wouldn't be a Porsche or anything like that. A Porsche would rust eventually, and then I would wish I'd asked for the thing I've always wanted – always.

You'll find out what it is at the end of this poem.

Christmas

Christmas happens anyway – it happened in our house
   today,
It's good! And yet, I have to say, for me there's something
   missing.
It's not that Santa didn't come; he floated past our worldly
   locks,
He drank his sherry, ate his pie, left me a pair of purple
   socks,
And lots of other things.
My daughter gave me half a beetle in a box, a touching
   sacrifice.
There's no significance, I hope, in all the gifts of scent and
   soap,
In mutant ninja turtle shapes!
And who sent exercising tapes?
That isn't very nice.
My son said, "Dad, I've spent a lot,
A portable word processor."
I really was excited till I got,
My pencil in a plastic pot.
But there were toys and Garfield mugs
And boxer-shorts and laughs and hugs,
And anyway, they always say, the thought's the thing that
   really counts.
There's something missing, and it isn't here. I'm not sure
   what it is.

The crib confuses me because – I see it as it surely was,
Divine confusion, shepherds visiting the new-born shepherd,
Mary proud but puzzled, Joseph close, concerned for her,
And what would tiny babies want with gold and
   frankincense and myrrh?

Why did a million angels fill the sky, like snowflakes on a
　　starry night?
I guess that no one quite knew what was going on,
Except that something *right* was happening,
And God was saying, and is saying still,
"Here is my son, do with him as you will.
Though you may kill him he will live for you forever now,
Not lost in rhymes or mimes or special times,
But in the human heart, where revolutions really start,
And struggles in the darkness never seem to cease.
He offered then, he offers now, the only gift you'll ever
　　want or need,
The possibility of peace."

Jane Drain

This is the first of five short sketches involving a writer,
that you will find scattered through this book. The first one
highlights the difficulty of being truthful with a person who
appears to have the direct authority of God on her side.

What *do* you reply to someone who says "The Lord told
me . . ."?

Jane Drain

W: = WRITER
G: = GUEST

W: Now, Miss Drain –
G: Call me Jane
W: Jane Drain – right. Err . . . Jane, you wanted to see me
　　to ask advice about writing. Yes?

G: Yes, well you're a writer aren't you?

W: (*Modestly*) Well . . . yes, I am.

G: The Lord has given me some poems (*She plonks a huge pile of papers on the table*) and in my quiet time last week he told me that *you* were going to help me get them published.

W: He, err, he's given you a lot, hasn't he?

G: Yes, and you're going to help me get them published.

W: Well, I'm not sure –

G: I get them all over the place.

W: What?

G: Poems. I never know when one's coming. I'll be lying in the bath –

W: (*Warily*) Mmm . . .?

G: And one just comes into my head and I have to jump out of the bath, all dripping and unexpected, and run round the house looking for a biro, and when I've found one I put it down quickly.

W: What?

G: The poem. I put it down as quick as I can.

W: When you say the Lord gives you these poems, Jane, do you mean –

G: Here's one I did this morning (*Takes sheet from pile*) It hit me in the shower when I wasn't expecting it. (*Reads*)

> When I into the Bible do look
> I think to myself what a jolly good book
> And there will be considerable joy
> For those who do it read, girl or boy
> In it we do learn that man a menace is
> Disobeying God since not far into Genesis
> Why do not we all ask God for his bounties
> Whether we hail from Scotland or the home
>   counties?
> Let us now to God show all due deference

> In ways relating to our denominational preference
> That way we might avoid a schism,
> This was revealed to me in the shower which is a bit
>   like baptism.

W: Well! That was . . . well!

G: What did you think?

W: Only *you* could have written that, Jane.

G: Which publisher shall we send my poems to, then?

W: Jane, the fact is that poetry, however, err . . . good, is just not a selling proposition.

G: Ah, yes, but these poems were given to me by the Lord, so they *will* sell, won't they?

W: Look, Jane –

G: I've written a little poem for you to read when you go out speaking and that (*Hands him a sheet of paper*).

W: (*Reads disbelievingly*)

> That I do write books there is no doubt
> Of thicknesses varied, some thin, some stout.
> In them I hope that I do capture
> The means by which we'll escape being left behind
>   when it comes to the rapture.

That's – very moving, Jane. Certainly moves me. Tell me, what exactly do you mean when you say that God *gives* you a poem?

G: Well, I'll be lying in the bath, and –

W: No – no. I mean what happens in your head?

G: I dunno – the words just pop into my head and then pop out on to paper. Anyway, which publisher shall –

W: (*Claps hand to head*) Just a minute, Jane! I think it's happening to me. Yes, there's a poem coming through, and I think it's for you. Listen –

Thank you for writing your poems divine
They're part of you, so I guess they're mine.
But frankly, Jane, it would make more sense
To publish a few at your own expense.

END

Wooden Man

I had a very negative view of Christianity until I went through a stress illness a few years ago. Having been converted at a time when, generally speaking, one was taught that God more or less held his nose as he allowed filthy repentant scum to slip, lizard-like, into his presence, it never really occurred to me that the creator was bothered about anything but stopping his verminous followers from pursuing their foul, sinful activities. It wasn't until I heard a sermon by John Collins on the subject of Jesus' parable of the sheep and the goats in Matthew, chapter twenty-five, that it began to dawn on me that Jesus is far more interested in what we *do* than what we don't do.

That sermon was a very important step in my journey towards understanding that, actually, God is nice and he likes me.

What follows is an extract from a production called *Coming Home* that I wrote for our local inter-church group. It is about the *positive Gospel* of Jesus, and I make no apology for the fact that it ends rather inconclusively.

Wooden Man

A. All I can think about is how rotten I am inside. There seem to be so *many* sins. If you get rid of one, another one pops up to take its place. I don't think I'll ever be good enough to do anything really useful for God.

B. Nobody's perfect, y'know.

C. Well, nobody except my friend Donald. He's never committed a sin in his life.

A. There isn't anyone who hasn't done anything wrong – is there?

C. My friend Donald hasn't.
   (*Pause*)

B. He's never done anything wrong? A perfect Christian?

C. My friend Donald – he'll be here in a minute so you can see for yourselves – he has never stolen, never murdered, never committed adultery, never envied, never lusted, never told a single lie, never been guilty of a cowardly act, never hurt anyone, never hit anyone, never hustled, harassed or hated anyone –

A. But surely –

C. Donald has never been greedy, slothful or avaricious, he's never dropped litter, disturbed the peace, driven with excess alcohol in his blood or destroyed other people's property. He's never had a single unkind thought, he holds no grudges, he never gossips, he's never late or lascivious or libellous. He has never caused, continued or condoned conflict of any kind. He never complains, he never blasphemes, he never gets drunk, he never overeats, he worships no false images, he's never mean or menacing or malicious –

B. But isn't that – ?

C. Donald never watches nasty videos, nor does he condemn people who do, he's never judgemental or over-sentimental, or harsh, or unforgiving. He's never sad, mad, bad or (*Hunts for words*) anti-oriental. He never smokes, he never swears, he's never rude, he never stares. Donald has never ever committed a single sin. Oh, and one other thing.

A. What's that?

C. He won't be going to heaven.
   (*Pause*)

A. Why not?

B. Because he's not very good company, I should think.

A. No, seriously – why not?
   (C. *Disappears and then reappears carrying Donald, a wooden figure*)

A. Because he's made of wood.

B. But you said –

A. You said he was the perfect Christian.

C. No I didn't – you said that. I just told you about all the things he's never done wrong. The trouble with old Donald here (*Pats him*) is that although he's never committed any of the sins I was talking about, he's never done anything else. He can't – he's made of wood. So – (*Looks at A.*)

A. So . . .?

C. So, it doesn't matter if you don't do anything wrong for the rest of your life. It won't make you a Christian and it won't get you into heaven.

A. What will then?

C. Now, that's a *very* interesting question . . .

Motivation

It's that writer again, only this time it's not Jane Drain he's having trouble with – it's himself. What really motivates him? Why does he do what he does? What a state he's in!

I remember asking a respected friend what he thought about motivation. He pointed out that when Jesus called Zacchaeus down from his tree he only wanted him to go and get the tea under way. He didn't demand an instant change of lifestyle; that came about as a natural progression from obedience. That seems to be the secret really. If you've been given a job to do, then get on and do it, and let God see to the fine-tuning.

Genuine obedience is just as much from the heart as more mushy things.

Motivation

W = WRITER
F = FRIEND

F: Hello, Rodney! You all right?

W: Hello, Viv – mmm, I've got a lot to be thankful for.

F: Oh, bad as that, eh? D'you want to stop rejoicing for a moment and tell me why you're looking so glum?

W: I dunno, Viv, I've been sitting here trying to write, and I suddenly thought – why am I doing this? (*Taps page*) Who actually wrote this stuff, me or God?

F: Let's have a look. (*Reads*) "Five pounds of potatoes, two and a half pounds of sprouts, six eggs and a packet of cornflakes." This is deep stuff, Rodney, I see your problem. Looks like your handwriting though.

W: Not my shopping list, you twit. I'm talking about my books –

F: Oh, sorry. Your books. Right.

W: I mean – *why* do I write books? I say it's for God, but is it? What's it for?

F: Money?

W: Oh come off it, Viv, you're not seriously suggesting

that I write about God for cash?

F: What do they pay you in, then – bananas?

W: No, but . . .

F: You told me the other evening – after your fourth glass of that wine you said was only slightly alcoholic – that you sift through the post every morning looking for cheques and you don't enjoy your breakfast much if there aren't any.

W: That was just the truth – I mean, that was just an exaggeration. You've got me confused now.

F: Maybe it's personal fame and glory, Rodney.

W: Maybe *what* is personal fame and glory, Vivienne?

F: Well, you know, the reason you write. Maybe you write so that people will think you're wonderful?

W: How long have you had this ministry of encouragement, Viv? Here, I didn't say anything about *this* after my fourth glass of wine, did I?

F: No.

W: Oh, good . . .

F: It was after your fifth –

W: Oh, blimey . . .

F: You said that, every now and then, you go down to the local Christian bookshop and look in the indexes of the new publications to see if you've been quoted.

W: (*Groans!*) Oh, I didn't say that, did I?

F: Was it true?

W: Well, it wasn't *untrue* . . . (*She laughs*) So you don't think there's anything good and pure motivating me to write?

F: I didn't say that.

W: No, but you've taken an interesting, sophisticated problem and reduced it to sordid issues of money and vanity. Blow you, Viv. I was really enjoying my problem till you came along.

F: Look, answer me two questions, Rodney.

W: (*Sulkily*) I don't remember having a sixth glass . . .

F: No – no, listen! Do you believe God wants you to write books?

W: Well – yes, I do really. Yes, I do, definitely – I think. No, I do! I *do* think he wants me to write books. Why?

F: (*Holds up shopping list*) Who's going shopping for this lot?

W: What?

F: Who's doing the shopping?

W: (*Shrugs*) Probably send one of the girls down. Is there something wrong with that?

F: No, but hadn't you better check her motivation before she leaves? Have you ever tasted sprouts bought by someone whose motives are mixed? Yuck!
(*Pause*)

W: Viv.

F: Yes?

W: Clear off – I've got some writing to do . . .

END

'Is this a motivationally deprived Sprout?'

Creed

Speaking at a local church a few years ago, I held up a jigsaw puzzle that had been specifically made for the occasion by a friend who is less ham-fisted than I am. It was the normal rectangular shape, but right in the centre of the puzzle was a large, tortuously shaped section that was nevertheless accommodated perfectly by the more orthodox pieces that surrounded it. Each of those surrounding pieces had needed to become a little bit irregular itself, but only on one side. I was making a plea for acceptance and tolerance of individual differences in members of the church community, and suggesting that the doctrinal frame of our faith is quite capable of holding and enclosing people as they are, and not as they should be.

Thank goodness God allows us to be what we are, and enables us to move towards becoming what we should be. We can be honest with him about the shape of our faith, even if it seems a bit irregular at the moment. One of my moments was shaped in the way that this poem describes.

Creed

I cannot say my creed in words.
How should I spell despair, excitement, joy and grief,
Amazement, anger, certainty and unbelief?
What was the grammar of those sleepless nights?
Who the subject, what the object
Of a friend who will not come, or does not come
And then creates his own eccentric, special dawn,
A blinding light that does not blind?
Why do I find you in the secret wordless places

Where I hide from your eternal voice?
I hate you, love you, miss you, need you, wish that you
would go.
And yet I know that long ago you made a fairy-tale for me
About the day when you would take your sword
And battle through the thicket of the things I have become.
You'll kiss to life a sleeping beauty waiting for the prince to
come.
Then I will wake and look into your eyes and understand
And for the first time I will not be dumb
And I shall say my creed in words.

STRENGTH AND VULNERABILITY

The greatest weakness is the fear of being weak.

French proverb

Strength and Vulnerability

Quite early on in my writing career I was asked to work at an event called "Take Seven". (I think this referred to the number of spare tents each family needed to have because the weather was so appalling. Later, this kind of Christian festival became the basis for the section on "Let God Spring Into Royal Acts of Harvest Growth" in *The Sacred Diary of Adrian Plass*.) Originally I had been asked whether I would be interested in fronting the evening chat-show, but my ideas on how this might develop were not very well received. Unfortunately I was not told this at the time. Instead, it was suggested that I would be much *more* useful in the capacity of seminar speaker on the subject of "Parenting". As an inveterate coward of long standing I have every sympathy with the person who curved the truth in this way. He is a charming fellow and I forgive him from the heart of my bottom. Besides, I learned a very valuable lesson down there in Shepton Mallet, as you will see.

Flattered by this implicit trust in my parental expertise, I agreed to address a large group of Christian mums and dads on the subject of bringing up children. It seemed quite easy when I was sitting at home not doing it, but as the date of the festival came closer and closer I began to panic seriously. What could have possessed me to imagine that I had anything remotely useful to say about raising a family? I reviewed my qualifications:

- I had been a child myself; but then, so had everyone else.
- I had been raised by parents. Big deal!

● I had three children of my own, but although I loved and liked them very much the whole business of family had been a Columbus-like voyage of discovery for me. There was no method in my madness.

True, I had dealt with children in care for most of my working life, but such skills as I had acquired in that field seemed to be non-transferable when it came to my own little children's home.

Dismally, I came to the inescapable conclusion that I had nothing to say on a subject concerning which those trusting mothers and fathers would undoubtedly believe I was some kind of expert. How naive I was then! Later, of course, I realized that if a Christian becomes well-known as an expert on – let us say – gardening, he will almost automatically be asked to speak about the theology of fuel injection. You just buy a couple of books, get some notes together, make sure they're heavily laced with relevant verses and Bob's your auntie! Anyone can do it. A lot do. I didn't know that – being so very green.

Then a new and awful thought struck me. My children would be coming along, all three of them, solidly present and visible evidence of the efficacy (or otherwise) of my platform philosophy. A waking nightmare took possession of my mind. There I would be, standing up at the front in a great big leaky tent, lecturing others earnestly on various aspects of fatherhood, when, suddenly, I would become aware that my audience was no longer listening. Instead, their eyes and attention would be fixed on the open tent-flap behind me, through which my offspring would be clearly visible – trying to kill each other on the grass outside. Grim-faced, I dismissed the nightmare and gathered my little darlings together. They sat in a row of three as I addressed them thus:

"Listen! Daddy's doing seminars on Parenting, right? So I don't want any trouble. Gottit?"

"Yes, yes, yes!" they all said, "we'll be good, of course we will . . ."

The time came, and we set out in our big old green Peugeot tank. The car was stuffed tight with camping equipment, food in cardboard boxes, children, sundry sporting accessories and quite a bit of rubbish from our last major trip. I don't drive. My wife, Bridget, drives. I navigate. My oldest son says this is like asking Cyril Smith to break the world pole-vault record. He's a very silly person sometimes.

The fact that we ran out of petrol fifty yards from the house didn't trouble me too much. After all, Bridget was the captain of the ship, as it were, so we could blame her, and we did.

Some time later, however, things began to get a little more serious. Bridget stopped the car, turned to me as I sat with the map on my knees, and said, "Adrian, why is the road getting so small? Why are we in a village called Funtington?"

The children had been singing, "We're off to Shepton Mallet! – we're off to Shepton Mallet!" Now they started to sing, "We've ended up in Funtington! – we've ended up in Funtington!"

All parents know how angry it is possible to get with children in a car. The vehicle turns into a ghastly red-hot oven full of sub-human fiends whose only talent is torment. I got furious with the children because I felt guilty, Bridget got furious with me because she thought I should be getting furious with myself instead of getting furious with them, and finally I took refuge in a sulk, hoping that by the time I came out of it everyone would have forgotten that it was my fault in the first place.

Whatever the ins and outs of this charming little domestic scene, by the time we arrived in Shepton Mallet the Plass clan was in a BAD state. As we passed through the main gates of the festival showground the lad who was

checking tickets enquired in the mildest of tones, "Are you speaking on something?"

"Yes," I growled back venomously, "PARENTING!"

I decided that the best way to restore harmony was to get the tent up, a good communal effort. Yes, you're absolutely right – I know nothing about camping *or* communal efforts. The strange, recently bought, aggressively heavy slab of canvas that we dragged from the back of our exhausted car bore no resemblance to any tent that I had ever erected. It was like a dead thing that had gone to heaven and didn't want to be bothered with coming to life again. When we did, at last, work out what was meant to go where, it was discovered that Daddy (me) had forgotten to include an essential pole. My family stood round in a circle and stared at me in the same way that people stare at some electrical appliance that has finally gone beyond repair. My oldest son went off and somehow managed to scrounge a spare pole that supported our tent (and our marriage) for the rest of the week. Glumness reigned.

By the time the morning came I was ragged. The thought of standing up in front of all those Christian parents was just too awful to contemplate. If you have ever had to tell people about God immediately after being vile to some close member of your family you'll know exactly what I mean. You want to die, but you can't.

Up I got, clutching a piece of paper on which were listed nineteen wonderfully shiny points about being a good father. I glanced at it before beginning to speak, and silently said to myself, "Well, you don't do any of them".

It was then that a little voice seemed to say, "What about telling the truth?"

"No," I said to myself, "we've managed without the truth in the Church for years. Why should I go and spoil it all now?"

But I decided to give it a go. I described to those present the events of the last twenty-four hours. I talked about my bad temper and my sulks. I confessed that the last thing I felt qualified to do was to pontificate about parenting. I thought it might have depressed them, but it didn't. You should have seen their faces brighten! Obviously none of them were very keen on having their mistakes itemized in nineteen easy-to-understand sections! *I* wouldn't have fancied it either. What those people really needed was permission to be vulnerable, and my admission of failure had offered them exactly that. Being a parent can be so painful sometimes. The last thing most of us want or need is to be intimidated by the bright and flawless ones.

That experience at "Take Seven" was the beginning of an essential understanding that vulnerability is a strength rather than a weakness. That applies just as much to public ministry as it does to selling cabbages. Here comes the second batch.

Worry

Jesus was very hot on "not worrying", wasn't he? Storms, food, clothing, what to say when the time comes, nasty things that people say about us, death itself – these are just a few of the things we're not to get hot and bothered about. I suppose that if we had the same insight into things of the spirit that the master had, we would be all too keen to relegate this team of concerns to the foot of our table of priorities.

As it is, many of us are locked into constantly recurring patterns of worry, often about things that are almost certainly never going to happen. It's easy to say we shouldn't be troubled in this way, but how *do* we break these patterns and become free?

As usual (at least I'm consistent) I have no easy answers, only a couple of suggestions.

First, Jesus said that the truth (or "reality" as it can accurately be translated) will be the thing that sets us free. Perhaps a re-reading of the gospels, with some sleeve-pulling prayer, will give us new insight into what reality really means. Let's not be silly about this – nobody is going to abandon deeply ingrained habits of worry because someone says it's a bad idea. There has to be a genuine change of perspective and probably a touch of the spirit before anything radical happens.

Secondly, the "truth" demands that we look honestly at what our worries actually are. When we have faced them with (possibly) a little more courage than usual, we might talk to another person about them, and that might be the first step towards constructing a plan of escape.

Whole lives are wasted by worry – about the wrong things?

Worry

No burglars came again last night,
Just as they failed to come the night before
And for as many nights as I remember,
No burglars yet again
Although I listened, as I always do for them,
Once more they did not oil and ease the rusty bolt that
    holds the garden gate
Behind the shed beside the house,
Nor did I hear them moving in the yard at some heart-
    sobbing wretched hour.
It was the ticking of a clock upon my wall

That like the pad of evil steps a hundred feet
    away.
They did not creep inside,
Their blind-from-birth brutality reduced to stealth and
    whispers
Did not stand above me,
Were not there with threats and ugly promises,
Intoxicated by the scent of fear incontinent
Nor did they then, with weapons that I meekly placed into
    their hands,
Proceed to sever from my chilled insides
The screaming child who has evaded birth for so long now.
They did not come.
They were not here again last night
And what if they should never come?
A waste of nights – I might have slept
But if I had, I feel quite sure
They would have come, those burglars
Yes, they would have come.

Beams

I wish I didn't have such an appetite for gossip.

"Adrian, there's something I feel I have to say to you
about Mavis, but I'm very anxious that you don't feel I'm
just spreading stories around for the sake of it. We're both
fond of Mavis and I know your only concern will be for her
welfare. Are you with me?"

Oh, yes, yes, yes, yes, yes! A thousand times yes! Of
course I'm with you, whoever you are. Gimme the dirt on
Mavis and we can call it anything you like. I've put my
mature, non-judgemental, seriously-concerned expression
on, so let's get to it – what's she done, eh?

My wife, who is looking over my shoulder as I write this,

has just suggested that I'm being a little hard on myself.

"I agree with most of the negative things you write about yourself," she says (thank you very much, dear), "but you've worked hard on this gossip thing. I don't think you do it much any more."

"Unlike some people we could name, eh?" I reply.

She has left, slightly annoyed.

But Bridget is right, I think. Although the appetite remains, unabated, I have tried to make a habit of countering criticism with praise, and simply not co-operating with muck-spreading ploys. I still fall sometimes, but it hurts me so much when I hear about others doing it to me, that I don't want to do it to anyone else.

As far as the church is concerned gossip is a killer, one of those noxious dark fluids that ooze in to fill the vacuum created by absence of courage, security and reality. I read somewhere once that gossip is a psycho-social necessity. I'm not sure what that is — but I don't agree. It's a bad thing.

Beams

A: Just between the three of us
            There's something I should share
            It's in the strictest confidence
            And purely for prayer
            But I just saw young Martin Spence
            With Mrs Falloway

B: You mean they're having an affair?

C: You told us he was gay

A: I think he was until last week
            But now the healing touch
            Has reached him through our loving prayers

C: We must have prayed too much

B:	I really like old Martin
A:	I think he's great –
B:	Me too
A:	It's such a shame he's lost control
C:	He sometimes has a few
B:	But we don't condemn our brother
A:	No! As one we sink or swim
	We've all been down that sinful road
C:	But not as far as him . . .
	Hey, Martin, fancy seeing you!
B:	Glad you made it, mate!
A:	We've been unholding you in prayer
MARTIN:	I'll tell you why I'm late.
	I've just been down the hospital
	With Mrs Falloway
A/B/C:	Ah!
MARTIN:	Her husband's in for treatment
	And she's visiting today
A/B/C/:	Oh!
MARTIN:	But listen – just in confidence
	And purely for prayer
	You know the place where people wait
	Well, guess who I saw there.
A/B/C/:	Who?
MARTIN:	Well, who believes that Christian folk
	Should not be sick or ill?
	Who would use a drop of oil
	Where others use a pill?
A:	Mildred Smith!
B:	A godly lass!
A:	Her faith is sure and strong
B:	She's full of hope and charity
A:	She's good
B:	She's kind
C/MARTIN:	She's wrong.
A:	Ah, Mildred, what a nice surprise!

	You're just in time for prayer
MILDRED:	I've just come from the hospital
MARTIN:	I know – I saw you there.
A:	Something wrong then, Mildred?
B:	We're concerned
C:	Allay our fears
MILDRED:	I visit there on Wednesdays
	I've been doing that for years.
MARTIN:	Oh!
MILDRED:	But if we're lining up for prayer
	Here's something for the queue . . .
A:	Is it something confidential?
B:	Is it just between us few?
MILDRED:	Yes, the vicar's looking desperate
	That man is never free!
	What with services and visiting . . .
C:	He never visits *me*.
MILDRED:	He told me he's exhausted
	But he doesn't want it known
A:	No!
B:	Of course not!
MARTIN:	We'll be very careful
C:	Where's the nearest phone?
A:	Let's pray!
B:	Oh, Lord, protect us!
C:	Don't put us to the test
MARTIN:	Forgive us all our trespasses
ALL:	As we forgive the rest.

Postmen

If we're going to be all metaphorical now, and it looks as if
we are, then I have to say that my wife has been the most
important "postman" in my life.

When Bridget and I did an evening together in the theatre tent at Greenbelt '91, the show was entitled "Mrs Plass and her husband".

Bridget came on first and recited the following lines:

Behind the greatest men, they say,
A woman humbly stands,
Her task to serve the genius she wed.
In all my girlish dreams,
I longed to be with such a man,
But then I married Adrian instead.
Perhaps I lack humility,
Perhaps I am too proud,
But if I were to stand behind him here,
The bountiful excess,
With which his stomach is endowed,
Would fill the stage and I would disappear.
The questions get me down,
How's Gerald? Are the Flushpools real?
I like that monk,
Is he a local man?
Exactly why was Leonard Whatsit borrowing the cat?
And how come you're called Bridget, and not Anne?
To those of you who feel
(And there are some of you who might),
That being Mrs Plass should thrill my heart,
He has a ghastly habit,
That would give you quite a fright,
It's —

At this point I made an appearance on stage just in time to cut short the awful revelation. But that bit of nonsense had some truth in it. Bridget has been an immeasurable source of support and strength as far as I'm concerned, and quite apart from putting up with those ghastly habits that she nearly mentioned, she has been the most reliable postman of all in my life, delivering common sense and the heart of God to me on so many occasions.

And now it's time for me to come out of the closet and confess to my post habit. Be strong – it's not a pretty story.

Postmen

I have become a post junkie. I can no longer live without my daily fix. Sundays are a nightmare. What will become of me?

It's not even as though I like much of my post when it does come. Bills are nasty, circulars are boring, letters asking why I haven't replied to the last two letters are guilt-inducing, and invitations to come and collect my prize at a local hotel from time-share salesmen drive me into a wild frenzy.

So why do I begin to salivate mentally at eight-thirty each morning? Why do I pace restlessly to and fro by the window of the upstairs sitting-room and gaze yearningly up the road in the direction from which the postman usually comes? Why, when the dog goes berserk and the letter-box clatters, and the mail lands with a muted thump on the front mat, does my heart leap up with joy and anticipation? I suspect that part of the answer lies in the random quality of post – anything could come from anywhere and anyone. It is a regular source of potential unexpectedness in a life which, with four children at school, is necessarily as ordered as people like us can manage.

It is also, as my oldest son would be quick to point out, because I am prone to developing loony obsessions. This same oldest son, knowing how I pant like a thirsty dog for my daily epistolary dose, will sometimes sprint to the front door before I can get there, scoop up the mail in one well-developed movement, and retreat to his bedroom. There, behind hastily erected barricades, he can enjoy the scratching, whining and bloodthirsty threat-making that emanates from his sad, demented father as he laments for that which he has not got. One day I shall push *him* through the letter-box.

My mania reached new heights at a past address when it began to seem to my feverish imagination that different postmen were bringing different kinds of post. The same part of me knew that this could not possibly be so, of course, but sometimes the evidence appeared to be overwhelming.

There were three postmen.

The first, and most regular one, was a grandfatherly older man with kind eyes and a relaxed, benevolent aura. He pushed a trolley around his "walk", as I believe it is called, and he never seemed to be in a hurry. This excellent postman could be relied upon to bring fat cheques, warm letters from old, dearly loved friends, and invitations to dinner parties with people we liked. A Father Christmas of the postal world, he had nothing but goodies in his sack.

The man who regularly brought the second post was a different type altogether. He was very much younger for a start, no more than nineteen or twenty, and he conducted himself with a carelessness that bordered on flippancy. Often, from my post at the upstairs window, as the time for second post approached, I would see this lightweight young person swinging round the corner at the top of our road on his bicycle, and watch as he then pedalled along the straight stretch with his hands off the handlebars and a dreamy smile on his face. I would have laid heavy odds on his being involved with an unskilled but highly ambitious rock band.

The post he brought was pathetic – predictably so. He brought vouchers offering 10p off well-known makes of washing powder; large, impressive-looking envelopes with huge print screaming that you'd probably won £50,000, only you knew you hadn't; unsealed brown envelopes containing the quarterly bulletin of the Retired Gentlefolk's Association and addressed to the person before last who lived in your house. He just didn't try. He wasn't cut out to be a postman.

The third one was the worst of all! He filled in when the older man was ill or on holiday, and I dreaded his coming. Small, thin, horribly clean and unremittingly severe in his manner, he was, we happened to know, a member of the small but very stern religious group that met every Sunday in a little corrugated iron hut at the other end of the town.

During the weeks when he delivered to us the supply of fat cheques and warm letters simply dried up. I know why – they would have been bad for us. Instead, he brought knife-edged envelopes containing bills that were red with anger, postcards from the public library demanding the return of their books, letters from the bank charging fifteen pounds to point out that we hadn't any money, and ranting communications from members of obscure sects who, having read and disapproved of one of my books, wanted to point out that I would spend an eternity of misery with Satan unless I spent a lifetime of misery with them.

He was a terrible postman!

So what is the point of all this? Well, it's very simple really. I was wrong about the three postmen. It was just a fantasy. They all brought the same selection of post because they were all employed by the same firm. Howeer much I may have wished it otherwise, their character and temperament were irrelevant to the items that they actually delivered.

Sometimes I'm tempted to ignore or discount ministry that's offered to me through an individual or a church that isn't to my taste or liking, especially, in my case, if it's someone who is familiar and close to me.

Let us beware! God sends the messages *and* he runs the entire delivery service. The rest of us are just postmen.

Graces

I was rather pleased when a friend rang to ask if it would be possible for me to write a "grace" to be said before the meal at a local gathering of Licensed Victuallers. What a pleasure it was to produce something for a group of people who have probably never heard of Graham Kendrick – or Adrian Plass, for that matter.

What a lot of colour and life we miss by avoiding what we suspiciously refer to as "the world".

I was severely handicapped, of course, by my profound ignorance of alcoholic drinks, but after much anxious thought I suddenly remembered my friend, Eric Delve, mentioning that he had once had a small port in a Public House in Godalming. I hastened to ring him, and to my relief found that he recalled the incident quite clearly. What a memory he has! Even after such a great lapse of time Eric was able to recollect the names of several drinks that had been bought by other patrons of the bar.

Off I went, but after completing the Licensed Victuallers' Grace I got a bit carried away and did one for taxi drivers as well. The mania had me in its grip by the time that one was finished, and I steamed ahead with something suitable for British Rail employees. When my wife came in I looked at her with crazed eyes and held up a list of fifty or more different occupations.

"Look," I said, "I'm going to write a grace for every single one, even if it takes – "

"Three's enough, I would think", said my wife.

Here they are. I'm going to do some more when she's not looking.

Graces

1) FOR PUBLICANS:
Lord, we meet together here,
Mild and bitter, stout and pale.
Grant, from now till final orders
That our spirits never ail.
With specific gravity
We shall hock depravity,
Please fill each hungry cavity
Let gratitude prevail. Amen

2) FOR TAXI-DRIVERS:
Simple thanks we offer now,
No trace of ambiguity,
For once we'll take this humble fare
Expecting no gratuity. Amen

3) FOR BRITISH RAIL EMPLOYEES:
Speed this food, Lord, as it comes
On its journey to our tums.
Let there be no long diversion
Of this edible excursion,
Unavoidably delayed
Just behind the shoulder-blade,
Or stranded in the lower back
By lettuce leaves upon the track.
May all traffic safely pass
And our digestions be first-class. Amen

Lewis and I

You may have some difficulty in believing that the little story I'm about to tell you is true. I can understand that, but try to fight this lack of trust within yourself. Above all, please don't get the idea that I'm just cashing in on the Lewis industry as so many other people have done. We Christian writers are not afraid of our personal limitations, you know. Ha! The very thought.

After all, I *might* have met him.

Can you prove I *haven't* met him?

He was alive during my lifetime so I *could* have met him.

Were you there when I *didn't* meet him? (Not that I didn't – I did.)

Anyway, if that's the way you feel, nobody's *making* you read it.

Oh, go on – read it.

Lewis and I

I thank God that I am more restrained than other men.

Despite a flood of highly attractive offers from major international publishers I have, until now, refused to describe or discuss the intimate details of my encounter with C. S. Lewis. The memory is sacred to me, and were it not for the specific leading that I have recently felt, I would have quite happily taken my secrets to the grave.

It was, then, on a cold and blustery autumn afternoon in Oxford, as I was in the very act of purchasing a fresh cream doughnut in a small but interesting baker's shop near the centre of town, that I suddenly espied the great thinker and writer standing in the doorway of a shoe-shop on the opposite side of the road.

I was transfixed, as you may imagine, for the entire ninety seconds that elapsed before a car drew up and transported the creator of Narnia away to some other world. Hardly able to believe what had just happened, I took a pen from my pocket and begged a paper bag from the girl who had been serving me. Impressed perhaps by the luminous urgency of my expression, she pushed one into my hand and retreated into some back room or area of the shop.

That paper bag, covered in hastily scribbled notes, lies before me now, evoking memories as fresh as the cream in that distant doughnut, long ago consumed, but never to be forgotten.

Lewis was standing (my notes inform me) with his weight evenly balanced on both feet – and how fitting that was! One foot in fantasy and one foot planted, with exactly equal firmness, in the reality of what *is* and cannot be ignored or changed. It was the balance also between academia and that – oh, so profitable awareness that great truths must be taught with great simplicity by great minds. One would not wish to read over much significance into random events, but it seemed to me that there was what I can only describe as a sort of parabolic synchronicity in Lewis's decision to position himself in front of an establishment that sold footwear. For he himself was responsible through his writings for providing so many folk with the winged sandals, not of Hermes, but of free and unburdened access to the things of God. (It is interesting to note that immediately after Lewis's departure – the shop closed!)

Tears and jam blur a part of my next note, but the picture in my mind is too clear for recollection to fail. Lewis extended his right hand – palm upward – and gazed at the sky for a full five seconds or more.

Yes, the storm clouds were gathering, and yes, the

first fragmentary drops of October rain (God's "natural baptism" as G. K. Chesterton called it) were steadily beginning to fall on that hand whose sure grip had already penned so many and such varied works of literature.

In that moment I seemed to see both a resistance and a submission in Lewis's response to the wild weather of adversity, criticism and self-doubt. He did up one button of his jacket – but *only* one. He frowned slightly towards the clouds, but almost immediately withdrew even further into the shelter of the shop doorway, perhaps seeking in an instinctive way the surrounding comfort of those symbols of individual progress that thronged the windows on both sides of him. From, as it were, the casemented warmth of popular affirmation he would be able to emerge fearlessly (Lewis was *not* carrying an umbrella) into the inclemency of disapproval and difficulty.

Engorged with the richness of these unique insights, my doughnut still untouched, I hardly dared continue to watch as the final act of this fascinating drama began to unfold. Without any warning Lewis lifted his left wrist, cupped his right hand around his watch, and peered intently at it for a second or two before raising his head and nodding, as if to say: "Yes, it *is* time."

And, of course, it *was* time. It was Lewis's time. It was my time. It was and is and will be the time of those generations who have and shall and must benefit from the offerings of such a genius. It was with a smile of infinitely sweet sadness that Lewis greeted the arrival of the vehicle he was awaiting, a smile that bade farewell to the *then*, welcome to the *now* and patient resignation to the *not yet*.

It was a privilege to be there on that day, and it surprises me not one iota that responses to the leaking of this unique experience have been uniformly negative. Already an article has been published in America, claiming that Lewis was speaking to an audience of hundreds in a completely different country on the day in question, but that, I fear, is the voice of jealousy braying across the Atlantic.

Next year I plan to publish a paper examining the style and content of a note left by Lewis for his milkman in the late fifties. I believe in my heart that this recently discovered document will establish beyond all reasonably doubt that C. S. Lewis wrestled with an obsessional desire to control the working habits of others.

True scholars could not be other than appreciative.

Angels

I know very little about angels. I know that they are God's messengers – more than messengers. I know that they fight, and comfort, and protect, and that we might entertain them unawares.

I know also that they would like the opportunity to become sons and daughters of God – the opportunity that *we* have.

I wonder if it takes some of them a while to accept their limitations? Do you think God will forgive me if I undertake a brief, whimsical conjecture? I hope so, because here it comes.

Angels

Two angels were gossiping in the waiting-room of the buckshot clinic.

"I don't complain," said the larger one, "because I'm an angel, but if I wasn't I'd have something pretty sharp to say about the allocation of names to us heavenly beings. It's all right if you're called something like 'Gabriel' or 'Michael'. They've got a real ring to them."

"What are you called then?" asked the smaller angel.

"Pongo – that's my name. No wonder I didn't get any mention in the boss's book. 'The Angel Pongo appeared to Mary . . .' Doesn't quite have the same impact, does it? What's your name?"

"Biggles", replied his companion sadly. "My name is Biggles – forever."

Silence descended as the two angels contemplated an eternity of ignominious nomenclature.

"And another thing," said Pongo, after a minute had passed, "I was on that angelic sub-committee that was supposed to ratify the boss's plans for his son's visit to the third planet. They gave me that Prodigal Son story to comment on. But did they take any notice of what I said?"

"Well, did they?" enquired Biggles with real interest.

"Did they, heaven! You've seen the final draft. I would have been furious, if I was capable of negative responses. I put in a very full report. Look, I said, the whole thing needs tightening up and refocusing. First of all, there's the road that this prodigal's travelling on. It's so vague! Anyone would think that the boss is willing to travel down any old cart-track that these human wrecks come staggering up

once they've realized which side their bread's buttered on. Narrow it down! That's what I recommended. Spell it out! Create an orthodoxy! Pin 'em down!"

"They didn't listen?" Biggles shook his head sympathetically.

"If I was capable of criticism," said Pongo, "and the boss was less than perfect, I'd say that this story embodies the kind of flabby liberalism that makes life so difficult for us angels. Why does the father come rushing down towards this wretched son of his while he's still a long way off? It gives the game away – that's what I said in my report. Why not let the kid do the whole trip? Keep him worried and guessing right up to the point where he reaches home. Then leave him standing at the door for a few minutes. Let him stew. Send the least important serving girl to let him in, and when he does finally get to see his father, let the old man be distant – a little bit cool. The son has to earn his way back into his dad's good books. That's what I suggested."

"Instead of which . . .?" coaxed Biggles.

"Instead of which," continued the larger angel, "we have what is (let's be frank) this embarrassing portrayal of the boss going for Olympic gold as he sprints down the highway with a bag of presents, like Father Christmas on jet-propelled roller-skates. Too vulnerable!"

"Too obvious," nodded Biggles.

"Too easy," asserted Pongo.

"Too emotional," added Biggles, rather absently.

"Too generous," declared Pongo, really enjoying himself now.

"Too wonderful," said Biggles dreamily.

Pongo frowned and shifted in his seat. "I might as well have not bothered sending in a report at all," he muttered. "Why deliberately provoke those Jewish humans by having the prodigal end up working with the pigs? That's another of the points I made. Then there's the cultural context. What happens, I wanted to know, when we reach the twentieth century, and people start calling it The Parable of the Failed Father? To my mind the boss was laying himself wide open. Two failed kids. Poor parenting. See what I mean? And why so tough on the older brother anyway? Poor bloke, slogging away – doing his best without so much as a thank you. No wonder he wasn't very pleased when his dirty-stop-out brother got all that V.I.P. treatment. If I'd been him I'd have had something to say about – just a minute!"

He looked narrowly at his fellow angel.

"What?" said Biggles, innocently.

"You just said the idea of the boss running down the road was 'too wonderful'. That is what you said, isn't it?"

"Well," said Biggles, turning slightly pink, "I was just thinking that, *if* I was capable of feeling envious, I might have wished that I could walk up the road like the prodigal and see the boss rushing down towards me looking all excited and throwing his arms round me and giving me all those gifts and throwing a party for me and telling me he loved me and – and all that. He's crazy about those humans, isn't he?"

Pongo looked into his companion's shining eyes for a moment, then sighed and smiled a sad little smile.

"Yes," he said quietly, "I suppose that if I had been capable of feeling envious, I might have envied . . . all that."

Positive Graffiti

Once or twice people have suggested that I am too negative about life, the Church, and everything. It hurts me to say this, but they may be right. Some good things have happened in my life.

So here, to make the people who've suggested I'm too negative feel good, and to earn me an extra blessing for listening to criticism and acting on it, is – (*Roll of drums*) something positive!!!!

Positive Graffiti

I have discussed elsewhere they way in which Satan uses his infernal aerosol spray to cover our hearts with graffiti. Jeremiah said that God will write his law on our hearts, but where these devilish scrawlings are too deep and too numerous to be easily erased, it can be a very long time before the Holy Spirit finally completes the cleaning job and enables us to present a clean sheet to the divine scribe.

Abuse, harsh words, ridicule, failure, rejection – the devil's negative graffiti come in many different forms. Sometimes a few words, not intentionally harmful but thoughtless and ill-chosen, can cause a wound that takes years to heal, and leaves a scar that never quite fades. How dangerous the tongue is!

It occurred to me recently, though, that, in my own life at any rate, there have been correspondingly positive experiences, events and influences that have counteracted or even replaced some of the negative ones. These heavenly graffiti come in many different forms, often through agents who have no specifically Christian connection. They are little gifts from God that may have a disproportionately profound effect.

I can remember three without really trying.

The first happened when I was about five years old and attending the little infants school in the village of Rusthall, where I was brought up. I was a slightly worried child, not particularly naughty, but given to occasional outbursts when I felt driven into a corner. One day I did something naughty in the playground, halfway through the dinner hour. I can't remember exactly what it was that I did but I do recall my awareness that it was "a fair cop". I was for it! The lady who was on playground duty dragged me into the top classroom and left me there while she reported my crime to the headmistress. When she came back she told me I was to wait on my own until the head sent for me.

I was terrified. My hair stood up and my blood drained down. What tigers there were in this jungle of a world!

At last the headmistress appeared at the classroom door and beckoned me to follow her through the corridor and into her office. I stood facing her as she sat behind her desk. I felt my bowels move ominously. What was going to happen?

After a moment's silence the headmistress pointed to a bowl on her desk and said, "Come and sit down and have some ice-cream Adrian".

She picked up a second bowl, and we sat, side by side, eating ice-cream together. She never mentioned my dreadful misdemeanour, and I certainly wasn't going to bring it up. I didn't feel any satisfaction about "getting away with it". I was just puzzled and surprised and relieved to find that authority did not exclude mercy.

The second experience happened just outside Paddington Station in London. I was a raw, unsophisticated teenager, anxious to project a cool, confident image to the rest of the world. A porter carried my bags from the train on which I'd travelled, to the bus-stop just up the road from the station. As he bent down to put my luggage on to the pavement I felt in my pocket for some change. I knew what

to do now. When porters carried your bags you gave them a tip. How much? I didn't know – I'd never been in this position before.

Withdrawing my hand from my pocket I looked at the selection of coins. Airily I selected two florins (a florin was the same as a ten pence piece) and handed them to the porter, who was just straightening up. He stood quite still for a second or two, studying the two coins that lay in the palm of his hand, then, after a searching look into my face, he handed one of them back to me, and said, in a voice tinged with some mid-European accent, "Two shillings is quite enough".

Even I, naive as I was, knew how unusual it was for *anyone* to return any part of a tip. The porter had given me a little free lesson. It warmed my heart to know that his generosity extended to strangers. Perhaps he had a son of my age.

Thirdly, there was George.

George worked in a paint distribution warehouse near Bromley, a place where five or six employees plodded around behind metal trolleys, assembling orders to be delivered to retailers. It was a place of long alleys running between high shelving units, loaded with every conceivable variety of paint, a veritable maze.

George was not in love with his work; there was nothing very inspiring about piling tins on trolleys. In his mid-

forties and totally lacking in ambition, George was an
expert in the art of disappearance. He knew the alleys like
the back of his hand, and he spent the day playing hide and
seek with the foreman, a little, frantic man with no top
teeth who ran around the warehouse clutching a sheaf of
overdue orders in his hand, and plaintively calling for one
of the mole-like trolley-pushers to come and fill them.
Occasionally George allowed himself to be spotted in the
distance, passing across the far end of an alley, moving
with considerable speed, and looking as if he had suddenly
remembered where some obscure variety of paint was
stored. George was a master of the art of doing nothing,
and he did it all day.

I was working in the warehouse as a vacation job in
between terms at the teacher-training college in Bromley. I
was in my mid-twenties at the time. Unlike George, I

worked very hard at assembling orders, mainly because it was so excruciatingly boring if I didn't. George and I got on very well, though, and one day he saved me from death by tedium.

At that time I was a fairly heavy smoker. It was one of the few things that made life in the warehouse bearable. One day I left my packet at home and was quite desolate. With no money to buy any more I steeled myself to an eternal, cigarettte-less day.

George, also a smoker, realized my predicament, and throughout that day, found me at regular intervals, handed me a cigarette without speaking, and returned to whichever bolt-hole he was occupying at the time.

Leaving aside the rights and wrongs of smoking, it struck me then, and it strikes me now, that George, with his redundant teddy-boy haircut, and his rather grey aimless view of life, did a very sweet thing for a fellow human being on that day.

My headmistress, the porter from Paddington Station and generous George, each offered me, in their own way, the cup of water that Jesus talked about his followers needing. And each will undoubtedly receive the reward that he also mentioned.

Thank God for positive graffiti, and those whom he uses to provide them.

YOU, ME AND US

There is little less trouble in governing a private family than a whole kingdom.

MICHAEL DE MONTAIGNE, *Essays* 1580

If you wish to study men you must not neglect to mix with the society of children.

Ibid.

You, Me and Us

A few years ago we enjoyed a family holiday in Denmark, and I can testify that there's a lot more to that ancient kingdom than bacon and Lego. The eastern peninsula that we explored was beautiful to look at and full of interest. More importantly from the point of view of our three boys, there was a football pitch and two practice goals just up the road from our holiday house in the village of Stenvad. It was a comfortable place to stay, with a "cricket-sized" garden at the back.

We had some very silly jokes from some members of the family. Worst of all was the suggestion that when we got home we should take our films into the chemist, then when we returned to collect them a few days later, we would say, "May we have Hamlet, please?"

"Hamlet?", the shop assistant would enquire.

"Yes," we would reply, "the prints of Denmark."

Gettit?

The best thing, as usual, was just being together as a family, arguing in peace for once.

Sometimes the holiday ethos allows quite subtle problems to rise to the surface.

One evening, after the younger members of the family had finally been coaxed, threatened and bribed to bed, my oldest son put into words an area of concern that had never occurred to me. He described how, as he listened to Bridget and me talking to the younger children, praising them for things they'd said or bought or done, he recognized in the words we used and the tone of our voices, the same kind of encouragement that had enabled him to feel valued and approved of as *he* grew up. Now, however, seeing how positive we were about quite small efforts and achievements on the part of the little ones, he started to feel a little insecure. Perhaps we had been less than sincere when we praised *him* in the past. What if his feelings of allrightness were based on a series of half-truths? Maybe we weren't really proud of him after all.

I didn't really know what to say in reply to this, but by the next morning the issue had resolved itself into a question in my mind: Which is more important in relationships – the love of truth, or the truth of love?

Should our response to the efforts of others be doggedly, uncompromisingly accurate, or should we let love mould and modify our reactions.

I tried to explain what I was thinking to my son, but it was only when I got down to concrete examples in his own life that he began to see what I meant.

"What about you with Katy?" I said (Katy was three and her biggest brother was potty about her). "What about when Katy brings you one of her drawings and asks what you think of it? Do you say, 'I'm sorry, Kate, but it's just a meaningless scribble'? Or do you say, 'Well done, Katy, that's really lovely!'? In fact," I went on, seeing his face soften, "would you be happy if you knew that the way I feel about you is the same as the way you feel about Katy?"

"Yes," he said "I would."

"That's good then," I said, "because it is."

The maintenance and repair of relationships with God, family, neighbours and fellow believers is an absolute priority in our lives, but what a tricky area this can be. I was about to say that this next cart-load of "cabbages" includes some ideas and issues that are rather personal to me, but I think I can safely say that most of us ratbags can easily identify with each other's problems.

So stay with me (unless your relationships are totally under control, of course).

Generations

G. K. Chesterton described atheism as a nightmare – a maze without an exit.

My own atheistic nightmare is concerned with the inexorable roll of the generations. So much birth and death and joy and grief, happening over and over and over like a constantly repeated film, in which only the faces change slightly each time. Grandparents who will probably never know their great-grand-children, and will certainly never know their great-great-grandchildren, and wouldn't be able to remember all their names anyway because there would be far too many of them.

"Oh, God, let it all mean something!" I have cried at those times when the darkness just won't go away. My heart would break if I ever seriously believed that all our relationships turn to dust. What would be the point of anything?

"Don't be afraid," said Jesus, "I have overcome death."

Generations

1)   I took my daughter to the park last night
      She ran with a shout to the roundabout
      The roundabout went round and round
      But it never stopped anywhere very profound
      It just went round and round and round,
      It just went round and round.

2)   I took my daughter to the park last night
      She bounced like a spring to the grown-up swing
      It swung quite high and it swung quite low
      But there wasn't any doubt where the swing would go
      It just swung high and it just swung low,
      It just swung high and low.

3)   I took my daughter to the park last night
      Her eyes grew wide when she saw the slide
      She climbed up the steps and she slid back down
      But the same sun set on the same old town
      She just climbed up and she just slid down
      Just climbed and slid back down.

5) We're all going down to the park tonight
    Where the swings go high and the swings go low
    But there isn't any doubt where the swings will go
    And you climb the steps and you slide back down
    While the same sun sets on the same old town
    Where the roundabout just goes round and round.
    And never stops anywhere very profound
    It just goes round and round and round,
    It just goes round and round.

Waste of Days

Our writer is in an even trickier position now than he was
before. Having sorted out the abominable Jane Drain, and
worked out where he stands on motivation, he is now
dead, and about to discover if the words he wrote so easily
in life will do him any good at the gates of Paradise.

I suspect, although never having been dead I can't be
sure, that God's idea of priorities may turn out to be very
different from ours. Poor old Rodney Fuller finds that the
books he's written are of far less importance than the way
he has treated his family, especially in his use of time.

Recently I have become very conscious of the richness of
days that most of us possess. So many mornings and
afternoons and evenings to use as we wish. We can
squander them or spend them wisely, and of course that
will mean different things to different people. Walking on
the Downs could be the best or the worst way to use a day;
helping a neighbour can be selfish or unselfish; working
without a break can be admirable or cruel. Our hearts tell
us the truth if we want to listen.

Which reminds me – I said I'd go and play snooker with
my son this evening.

Waste of Days

W = WRITER
A = ANGEL

W: (*Approaching desk*) Err . . . excuse me.
A: (*Brisk and pleasant*) Yes, sir?
W: Is this . . . heaven?

A: Front-desk, yes, sir. Did you want to come in?

W: Well, err, I'm a writer.

A: That doesn't automatically disqualify you, sir. We've admitted publishers before now. If I can just have your name.

W: My name's Rodney Fuller. (*No response*) I wrote Christian books. I've written lots of, err . . . Christian books. Are you an angel?

A: Yes, sir, I am an angel.

W: Well, I wrote a book about angels – a sort of novel – you know, about how things really are for angels.

A: (*Dryly staring*) Yes. I read it.

W: And I wrote another book called *Boldness before God: The Certainty of Salvation*. Err . . . do you think I *will* be allowed in?

A: I have your file here, Mister Fuller (*Studies it for a moment*) and all your books. (*Puts pile on desk*) These are all yours, are they not?

W: (*Encouraged*) Yes, yes they are. Writing was my ministry, you know.

A: Writing was your *obsession*, Mister Fuller. According to this file you robbed your family, your friends, your community and your church of a year and a half's worth of free time just so that *this* (*Holds up book*) could be written, for instance. (*Reads title*) *A Study of the Relationship between Hair-length and Heroism in the Pentateuch*.

W: That was described as "A very important book".

A: Yes. (*Consults file*) by the Latvian Christian Barbers In Exile Association's five-yearly news bulletin, which was only produced once because its seventeen subscribers had all died before the second edition was due.

W: Well, it was a bit of a minority –

A: And while you laboured away on behalf of seventeen octogenarian hairdressers your wife was putting the kids to bed, looking after visitors, cleaning the house, sorting out the bills, fending off door-to-door Spring Harvest salesmen, apologizing to needy people in the local community for your non-availability, writing an article about not having time to write a book, doing a part-time job, mowing the lawn, planting out vegetables, and putting up with your chronic bad temper – all because you had convinced her that you were engaged in the Lord's Work!

W: I was committed!

A: You were fanatical.

W: I was creatively absorbed!

A: You were self-indulgent.

W: I was spiritually driven!

A: You were an Anglican.

W: But I thought –

A: Mister Fuller, at birth your account was credited with sixty-nine years, three months and nine days. That is a very sizeable deposit. It has now been spent to the very last moment, and these records suggest that a large proportion of what you used to describe as your "writing career" involved the squandering of very valuable hours. Balance, Mister Fuller – that is what you failed to achieve – balance!

W: I'm not going to be saved by works, am I?

A: (*Pats books*) Well, not these, no. Up here, Mister Fuller, it's not what you've done or what you know, it's *who* you know.

W: (*Brightening*) I had tea with Eric Delve once.

A: I thought you *wanted* to come in.

W: I do, I was only joking. I – I know Jesus. I've written about him.

A: Oh! (*Examines file - pauses*) Well, let's hope he's written about you . . .

END

Today's News

I very rarely set out to be obscure in my writing. On the contrary, I can't understand why, in the vast majority of cases, writers would *not* want readers to know what they are getting at. I have to confess, however, that in the following lines, which are song lyrics, the images employed are quite deliberately selected with a view to offering the listener an impression of what I want to say, rather than a clear picture.

Why?

Good question. I suppose the answer is partly that I just enjoyed the freedom of communicating without accountability, and partly that fuzzy pictures can sometimes reveal more soul than photographs.

Having said that, some of the metaphors are quite obvious, and I promise that they all mean *something*. For instance:

> For her memory is blind
> To the one who touched her body
> In the middle of her mind.

This refers to child abuse, and the psychological mechanism that conceals painful memories from the conscious mind, but is unable to prevent the wounds caused by those forgotten events from festering, and poisoning the victim for years.

Can you work out what all the other images are about? Can you be bothered?

The general theme of the piece is that large-scale convictions, movements and principles, even if held and supported sincerely, are not much use if they never affect anything or anybody on a small scale. At least, I *think* that's what it was about . . .

Today's News

Today's news came on the wrong day
And the right day never comes
Though the man who is tied to the dragon
May smile as he does his sums
But he doesn't understand
That we just can't handle
The pain in the universe.
Someone'd better tell the man, he doesn't seem to care
If love's not down in the market square
It's not anywhere.
I'ts not anywhere.

The bear is called a pussycat
The cat's become a mouse
But it hasn't made a difference
To the feeling in our house
For mother's in the same old place
The baby's out the back
My brother hit the ceiling
Then he bounced into the crack
And the sun is getting hotter
And the sky is getting old
But the central heating's busted
So our feet are just as cold
It's not that we don't see the dead
A thousand years away
But there's someone in our upstairs room
Who might be dead today

Today's news came . . . etc

Would-be-good, the watcher
Wanted poetry in stone
But the valley of the dwellers
Is already overgrown
By the pestilence upon her
For her memory is blind
To the one who touched her body
In the middle of her mind
The icemen love experiments
But this will never do
For the maze is getting difficult
The rats are coming through
And the voluntary patient
Hates the pattern that he's known
For the shape of it is uglier
Than anything in stone

   Today's news came . . . etc

Somewhere there's a city
Where the washing powder's been
All the citizens are sleepy
And defiantly unclean
But in the solid cells
Behind another city wall
There are people who are clean and grey
And never seen at all
Fifty million babies
Have been planted on the moon
And another stepping-stone
Will be a mausoleum soon
But here we step more warily
Across the wild park
For the city's getting dangerous
The city's getting dark

Today's news came on the wrong day
And the right day never comes
Though the man who is tied to the dragon
May smile as he does his sums
But he doesn't understand
That we just can't handle
The pain in the universe
Someone I'd better tell the man, he doesn't seem to care
If love's not down in the market square
It's not anywhere,
It's not anywhere

Clay

One of the wonderful things about Christian marriage is that you never have any rows or arguments, so when I wanted to write about conflict in relationships I had to go round all my friends asking them if they could tell me what it was like. At last I found some people who remembered having an argument some years ago, and they have kindly allowed me to record the details of that event in this book.

And if you believe all that, you'll believe anything!

Arguments in marriage are like pieces of music – harsh music perhaps, but with familiar and oft-repeated tunes. It seems to me a legitimate function of drama that it should face people with the truth of what they do to each other. Maybe it might even help them to change the music – something a little more harmonious, perhaps?

We must be careful with each other. We are only clay.

Clay

W: Well?

M: Well what?

W: Aren't you going to ask me how I got on?

M: How did you get on?

W: Well, don't sound too interested, will you? (*Pause*) What's the matter?

M: Nothing. Why?

W: I dunno, you just seem . . . funny.

M: How did you get on?

W: (*Excited*) I actually made a pot! I made one! It weighs about three and a half pounds, and it only holds about a thimbleful of water, but it's a pot! My pot!

M: (*Dully*) I thought you didn't go on the wheel for the first few lessons, or have I got it wrong?

W: No, we don't.

M: Oh, don't we?

W: I made this one with my hands, just, you know, squeezing and shaping. It was quite sensual!

M: It was what?

W: The feel of the clay – it's lovely stuff to handle – all squishy and thick and soft.

M: I thought the idea was to acquire a practical skill, not to have sensual experiences.

W: Oh, don't be so grumpy, darling. You're not jealous of a lump of clay, are you? (*Imitates him*). "I thought the idea was to acquire a practical skill, not to have a sensual experience . . ."

M: I don't think doing impressions of me is particularly helpful, do you?

W: What *is* the matter with you? (*Pause*) Have you not had a very good evening? (*Waits*) Michael?

M: I've just been here. Haven't really . . .

W: I thought you'd enjoy being on your own for a while. Was the dinner all right? (*Pause*) You have had your dinner, haven't you?

M: I couldn't work out the thingy . . . I dunno, I just couldn't be bothered in the end.

W: (*Genuinely distressed*) Michael, that was a lovely dinner! I spent ages getting it ready. All you had to do was turn it up for half an hour then take it out. What do you mean you don't know how to do it? – you've done it loads of times! Why didn't you –

M: Look, I didn't have my dinner, all right! It's hardly the crime of the century, is it?

W: No, but it's meant to punish the crime of the century, isn't it?

M: Don't be stupid! I –

W: The only thing is, we're not quite sure what the crime of the century is, are we? At least, I'm not! Is it my torrid affair with a piece of clay, or is it just that I left you alone to wrestle with the terrible complexity of an oven switch? Or is it something else?

M: (*Strategic sigh*) I'm beginning to wish I hadn't said anything at all.

W: I'm sure you are. Because you haven't actually got any real grievance at all, have you? I thought we left all this sort of stuff behind ten years ago. I just couldn't *stand* it if –

M: *Overwhelmed*) Look, can we just forget about it now please? I'm sorry! I wish I'd never – I mean – I'm sorry!

W: (*Pause*) Do you want to hear any more about my pot?

M: (*Back in the driving seat*) Yes, go on.

W: Well, it's brown.

M: Mmm . . . (*Nods*)

W: And ugly.

M: Mmm . . . (*Nods*)

W: Like you . . .

M: Humph!

W: (*Quietly*) Especially when you get like you got just now. What was going on? Please tell me.

M: There's no point in telling you.

W: Why not?

M: Because you don't really want to know. It's irrational, and you don't like that. If I tell you what I feel you'll just tell me how wrong I am to feel it.

W: No I won't.

M: Yes you will. You always do.

W: Well, I won't this time. (*Pause*) Try me.

M: (*Unconvinced!*) All right – I feel hurt and upset and threatened by you going out and doing something that doesn't involve me, and being all bright and happy about it and talking about – sensual clay, and . . . well, that's about it really.

W: (*Shaking head*) How can you *possibly* feel that?

M: See what I mean?

W: I mean – I just don't understand how you can say that. We *talked* about me doing an evening class. You said you thought it was a good idea. You were the one who persuaded me to get on and actually do it. Now you're spoiling it!

M: Look, you asked me what I was feeling so I told you. I said you wouldn't like it because it's irrational. It *is* irrational! I know it's irrational. But I'm stuck with being who I am and what I am because of all the – stuff in my past and all that. I didn't choose to feel what I felt this evening; it was just there. If you hadn't asked me what was the matter, I wouldn't have told you, then we wouldn't have had a problem would we?

W: (*Temporarily conned*) I'm sorry, Michael. I didn't mean to stir things up. I was just upset that you felt — (*Pause*) Wait a minute! What am I talking about? It's just like the old days. I've ended up apologizing for what you've done to *me*!

M: What?

W: Well, you say we wouldn't have had a problem if I hadn't asked you what was wrong, but that's not true, is it? You were in your "Guess what's the matter with me" mode from the moment I walked through the door. All morose and moody and (*Whines*) "couldn't work the thingy on the oven so I didn't have any dinner". Poor little boy!

It's true, isn't it? You were determined to show me how miserable you were. Tell me the truth for once!

M: (*Apparently deeply hurt and offended*) Are you saying that I usually tell lies?

W: Oh, dear! Have I exaggerated? I do apologize. What a convenient thing to latch on to. We're not *talking* about *my* exaggeration. We're talking about you! When I first met you, you'd just emerged into the adult world with "A" Levels in sulking, self-pity and — (*Searches for a word*)

M: You can't think of a third word beginning with the same letter, can you?

W: I warn you, Michael! I'm not going back to all that. If I can't do things on my own without you trying to punish me every time . . .

M: Yes?

W: (*Quietly*) I don't know. (*Pause*) I'm going out. I can't stay here at the moment.

M: Where are you —

W: I don't know where I'm going. I've got my pot in the boot. I might go down to Brighton for a dirty weekend.

M: Don't be silly . . .

W: What, irrational, you mean? Well, I'm sorry, Michael, but it's all because of my dreadful past. I'm stuck with being who I am, you see, and you don't have to make any effort to control yourself. I thought you knew that. It's just unfortunate if it affects anyone else. Ring round the hotels if you want to find me. Just ask for Mrs Clay (*Pause*) Oh!! I'll see you later! (*Exits*)

M: Hmm (*Longish pause for thought*) I think I'll have some dinner . . .

BLACKOUT

I Know What You're Going to Say

It's dangerous to assume that we know all there is to know about a close friend or marriage partner. I once acted in a play featuring a married couple who disagreed about the type of house they occupied. She was convinced that they lived in a two-storey house, while he was adamant that it was a bungalow. He had refused to go upstairs for years, because it would prove her point.

This deliberately absurd situation amusingly high-lighted the stagnation that can occur when long-term relationships are reduced to a set of predictable, constantly repeated verbal and behavioural shapes. Whole chunks of personality are put into cold-storage because they never became part of the relationship pattern at an early stage.

I always find it so sad to see a couple sitting in a cafe or restaurant, especially on holiday, gazing blankly into the distance because there's no point in trying to communicate when you know exactly how your partner is going to respond. Yes, I know it's a good thing to be able to sit in companionable silence, and no, Bridget and I *don't* always talk animatedly in cafes and hold Wildean conversations in restaurants, but you know what I mean. So sad.

One of the ways in which I annoy Bridget is by suddenly saying, apropos of nothing: "Who are you?"

I do put it on a bit, but that occasional question is born out of the sudden, genuine realization that this person who is so close to me that I can hardly see her, is actually a quite separate, complex, total human being who I don't know half as well as I think I do. I find those moments rather exciting in a number of ways.

Heaven preserve my relationship with my wife, and with God, from the illusion that I can be totally sure what either of them is going to say.

I Know What You're Going to Say

WOMAN: John, I've been thinking.

MAN: Mmm?

WOMAN: I've made a decision.

MAN: Uh-huh?

WOMAN: I'm going to stop work in September.

MAN: Well –

WOMAN: I know what you're going to say. How are we going to manage on one salary? Well we did it before and we'll do it again. We're far too extravagant anyway. It'll do us good.

MAN: I –

WOMAN: It's no good coming out with that old line about "How are you going to manage without your holidays and little treats?" It really infuriates me when you say that. You're virtually accusing me of being a simple-minded bimbo, which, for your information, I certainly am not!

MAN: You –

WOMAN: Don't bother telling me I've got some secret reason for stopping work, either. I haven't, and, quite frankly, I take exception to your view of me as a devious, self-seeking female.

MAN: Could we –

WOMAN: No, don't try to smooth me over. You can't call someone a neurotic simpleton and then make it all right with a few glib phrases. No doubt you'll claim you "didn't mean it". Well, if you didn't mean it you shouldn't have said it! How would you feel if you'd come to me with a carefully thought through plan and just had it steamrollered? Because that's what you've done.

MAN: I –

WOMAN: No, please don't insult my intelligence by denying it, because I simply won't listen. You've had your say and now it's my turn! Or perhaps I don't get a turn. Well, I'm going to take it anyway. I've told you I want to stop work, but you didn't seem to hear me. Or rather, you did hear me, but all you could do was go on in your usual style about holidays and treats and not being able to manage. So negative as usual! You don't agree with me, so that's the end of that.

MAN: It's –

WOMAN: You don't have to say any more. I get the message. Well, all right – I *won't* stop work! But just you bear in mind that it was you who bullied me into carrying on.

MAN: When –

WOMAN: It's useless trying to back-track now. It's too late! You've got your own way, now you can live with it. Keep on slaving away! Those are your orders to the resident servant. Well, okay, I will. But I loathe you sometimes, and one day I'll find the words to tell you how much – if I ever get a word in edgeways, which is unlikely.

MAN: But –

WOMAN: I'm sorry, I don't want to hear any more. You may not have finished, but I have! I'm going out. Goodnight! (*Exit*)

MAN: If only I'd kept my mouth shut . . .

Navigation

Having undertaken to do a seminar on "Sex" at Greenbelt '91, I began to lose my nerve. What on earth was I going to say on this thorny subject? Parenting had been bad enough at Take Seven a few years previously, but Sex?

"I'll have to call in sick," I said to my wife, "I don't know what to say. I can't come out with all that old 'God created sex – it's a beautiful thing – but only within the context of marriage' stuff. It may be true but it's hardly original, is it? What am I going to do?"

"Calm down," said Bridget, "I'll think of something."

And she did.

"What is it", she asked a little later, "that we've had more rows about than anything else while we've been married?"

I went through a list of five or six things that it might have been, but they were all wrong.

"Come on!" said Bridget, "think hard. What is it that's brought us nearer to physical conflict than anything else?"

And then it clicked. Of course! How could I have been so slow? There was absolutely no doubt about the cause of our most virulent arguments.

MAP READING.

And not just us. I have got into a car before now with the most saintly couple you could hope to meet. Never heard so much as a raised voice from either of them. Then it begins.

"*Why* didn't you tell me there was a turning coming up?"

"Well, last time I told you there was a turning you got cross with me and said you didn't need to hear about every little wrinkle on the map!"

"For your information, that 'little wrinkle' we just

missed was our last opportunity to leave this road for the next thirty miles. Thank you very much, I *don't* think!"

"How you can be so unreasonable, I just don't know!" (SHE CRIES)

And so on, and so on . . .

"The thing is," said Bridget, "that vicars and curates and elders and ministers and people like that ought to counsel engaged couples on map reading. The sex would follow on naturally from that."

"Err . . . the seminar, Bridget?"

"Yes, well what you need to do is write a sketch that combines sex and map reading. We'll start the seminar with that."

So I did — and here it is.

Navigation

VICAR: Well, now, Sally and Slim, this is the last of our marriage preparation sessions. We've already covered an awful lot of ground —

SALLY: Metaphorically.

VICAR: Yes, metaphorically, we've already covered an awful lot of ground. Last week Slim shared with us that he couldn't actually recall asking you to marry him, Sally, and that he was profoundly horrified by the prospect of spending the rest of his life with you, to the extent that (and I think he put it rather picturesquely) he would rather be stung slowly to death by killer bees than face you over the breakfast table every morning for the next fifty years. And I think we sorted that one out okay last Thursday. One of those little worries that needs to be aired, and err . . . well done, you, for airing it.

Now, your turn this week, Sally, to throw up –

SALLY: Not literally?

VICAR: Not literally, no . . . err, your turn to throw up any little last-minute worries or problems. (*Pause*)

SALLY: Well, there was one thing, and – well it ruined my parents' marriage, so I wondered if we could talk about it.

VICAR: Of course we can, Sally. What is it? (*Pause*) Is it err . . . alcoholism?

SALLY: No.

VICAR: Err . . . finance?

SALLY: No.

VICAR: Exegetical incongruity?

SALLY: No, we sorted that out with a pair of curling tongs.

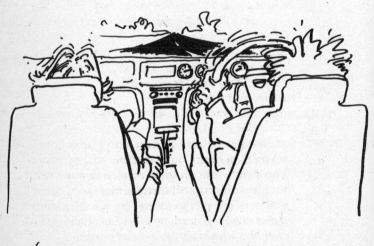

'If you took it more slowly Slim, the trip would be more enjoyable for both of us'

VICAR: Ah! So you're talking about –

SALLY: Yes, navigation.

VICAR: Yes, indeed, and I can tell you, Sally and Slim, that many marriages founder on the rock of navigational ignorance and conflict. Something that should be a natural and joyful experience can so easily end in trouble and tears.

SALLY: (*Tentatively*) We were wondering about (*Pause*) positions . . .

VICAR: Yes, well, traditionally the man – that would be you in this case, Slim –

SALLY: (*Taking out pencil and notebook*) Can I just make a note of that . . .?

VICAR: Traditionally, the man would sit in the driving seat, while the woman would sit in the passenger seat with the . . . map . . . on her knees. Nowadays, many couples prefer to do it the other way round, and there's absolutely nothing wrong with that. As long as both partners are comfortable and happy with what's happening, that's all that really matters.

SALLY: We're going to Leeds for our honeymoon in the car. Do you think we ought to navigate our way up there beforehand, just to see if we can manage it all right?

VICAR: I'm going to say the same thing to you as I say to all young engaged couples. It's perfectly proper to make short trips and excursions in the general direction of Leeds, but I must counsel you against going all the way at this stage. I think Milton Keynes is quite far enough. And once you get as far as Nottingham it's very hard to stop.

Times have changed, of course, since I was a young man. When I was driving out with a young lady it would never have occurred to me to leave Littlehampton, let alone attempt to navigate all

the way to Leeds. Not that I wasn't interested, I hasten to add. I well remember getting a terrible roasting from my father when he found a street map of Huddersfield hidden under my mattress.

Now, any other little questions or problems? Once you're married you'll gradually get to know each other's needs and it won't be long before you're reaching your mutual destination very harmoniously on every single occasion.

SALLY: We wanted to ask if it's possible when we actually start navigating to Leeds – I mean – if we get stuck at a junction, and Slim says it's my fault

for reading the map wrong, and I say it's Slim's
fault because he wasn't sensitive to the road
signs, and Slim says he wishes he'd never married
me in the first place, and I hit Slim with the
emergency flashlamp that we've asked Uncle
Vernon and Auntie Grace to buy us for a
wedding present, and we crash because Slim
temporarily loses consciousness, and we're on the
verge of giving up navigation altogether . . .

VICAR: Yes?

SALLY: Well, can you help us then?

VICAR: No, but I know a man who can, and he drives a
patrol car in the sky.

SALLY: Literally?

VICAR: Err . . . no, metaphorically.

SALLY: Thank you, Vicar. You're a very nice man. You're
a very, *very* nice man . . .

Dear Family

One of the pointless questions I ask myself from time to
time is whether I would opt for mental or physical pain if I
had to choose. It's difficult, isn't it – until you start to live
through one or the other, that is. Then you know for sure
that you would choose the kind of suffering that you are
not being afflicted with.

My own experience has been that, for years, I was quite
sure nothing could be worse than extreme physical pain.
After all, you can always find a way to distract yourself
from mental anguish. That's what I believed, and for most
of my early life it was true.

Then I had a family. They have brought me much joy,
but also the discovery of a new kind of pain; something to
do with observing the gradual death of innocence; even

more, I think, to do with my own shortcomings as a father
and a husband. Being a morbid beggar by nature I've
always made a bit of a meal of these things, but I have
known excruciating pain at times, and I've lost the knack
of distracting myself.

I'm sure that if I suddenly developed a chronically
painful illness, I would long for those good old days of
mental torment, but I still can't quite answer that original
silly question of mind.

I do feel sorry for Jesus at Gethsemane.

Family

Dear family, I write to you in this campfire place
Where temporary flames repel the savage things
Whose glowing, hungry eyes appear from time to time.
They know, as I do, that a campfire only burns as long as
    fuel lasts.
My stocks are low as ever, and these devils never rest.
But I have light and time enough to write to you
Dear family, asleep, for once, beside me here in peace,
To say how I regret the need to share such fearful travelling
    with you.
I know that monster-ridden darkness is my own affair
I have no right to take you there.
The battle I shall face tonight will threaten you
But certainly it never was your fight.
God knows I wish that it was otherwise
That we could strike our camp and head for home.
I have some choice
But when those creatures leap I find I am clean out of
    choice
And they draw blood so easily.
Dear family, as you awake,

And eye my campfire ashes nervously
I want to say how I am wretchedly aware
That others would protect and lead you properly.
They would be strong and confident and sure
They would be many things that I will never be
I only know they could not love you more.

REDUNDANT RITUALS
AND FLIMSY FASHIONS

Fools may invent fashions that wise men will wear.

THOMAS FULLER, *Gnomologia* 1732

Rituals, liturgies, credos, Sinai thunder: I know more or less the history of these; the rise, progress, decline and fall of these. Can thunder from all the thirty-two azimuths, repeated daily for centuries of years, make God's laws more godlike to me? Brother, no.

THOMAS CARLYLE, *Past and Present*, III 1843

Redundant Rituals and Flimsy Fashions

Some months ago I spent a morning at a small independent evangelical church in Kent. I was speaking about the need for each individual to experience the kind of explosively joyful encounter that we read about in the parable of the prodigal son; that moment when the father throws his arms round his returning offspring and showers him with love, forgiveness and a host of practical gifts. Trying to follow Jesus without that experience, I was trying to say, is difficult, if not impossible, because love is the greatest motivator of all.

After I had finished, everyone broke off into small groups (where would the Church be without small groups?), to discuss three or four questions relating to the talk. As they "discussed" I ambled around nervously, hoping that people were suitably stimulated and not sneaking covert glances at their watches every five minutes. Fortunately, all the groups seemed quite animated and had to be metaphorically prised apart so that we could enjoy our picnic lunch at one o'clock.

After lunch there was a brief feedback session (where would the Church be without brief feedback sessions?), and a short period of worship and prayer to round off the day.

"Good," I said to myself, as the last "amen" sounded, "I can relax now. The talk went all right, the discussions went well, the people were nice – time to go home."

It was as I lingered in conversation with a small group of elderly people at the back that I realized how miserably I had failed to convey my main point, at least as far as one person was concerned.

Her name was Beth, and she was one of those white-haired, attractive eighty-year-olds whose eyes are deeply crinkled from years of smiling. As I sat with Beth and two of her contemporaries someone mentioned outreach.

"I've always admired the old Sally Army," said the venerable gentleman on Beth's right, "the way they go into pubs and that with their papers. Maybe we should get to know people in the locals – then we could talk to 'em, couldn't we?"

"Not me," said Beth, the crinkles disappearing as she sat up a little straighter in her chair, "I would *never* do that!"

I looked at her for a moment.

"Suppose", I said, "that Jesus were to come through that back door now – today – and say 'Beth, I want you to come down to the King's Head with me.' Would you go?"

"I would not", replied Beth, compressing her lips and folding her hands together decisively in her lap.

"But, Beth," I persisted, "we're talking about Jesus, the son of God, asking you personally if you would go with him. Would you not go?"

"I have never set foot in a public house in my life," said the old lady adamantly, "and I'm not about to start now."

"But if Jesus himself asked – "

"It's a good witness," interrupted Beth, "alcohol has never passed my lips and it never will."

"Okay," I said, warming to my theme, "he doesn't want you to actually drink anything intoxicating, he just wants you with him in the King's Head, and – "

Beth shook her head firmly: "No!"

"Jesus, God himself, the creator of everything, the reason why we're all here today – he comes in and he says, 'Beth, I really need you to come to the pub with me today, so *please*, please make an exception, just for me.' Would you go with him?"

A tiny crack of uncertainty was undermining Beth's wall of principle. Her brows creased and her fingers twisted together as she mentally surveyed this rather unlikely scenario.

"I suppose", she said at last, "if he *really* did have a *really, really* good reason for asking, I *might* go."

Afterwards, as I travelled home, I thought about Beth and the way in which her principles seemed to be a more powerful motivating force than the relationship she had with Jesus. I realized that my own sticking points were often more personal than spiritual. Was I so aware of the love of God that I would follow him wherever he went? Or would I, like the rich young man in the Bible, go away sorrowing because there was some principle or issue or sin or religious habit concerning which I simply would not budge?

The alarming truth is that these "blocks" may well turn out to be respectable, laudable, even spiritual convictions or practices that have been elevated to the position of false gods.

Man-made fashions, fads and patterns can cause a lot of trouble as they work their way through the life of the Church. Here are quite a few examples in this last consignment of "cabbages".

Cabbages

I don't suppose God really minds what kind of spiritual activity we indulge in as long as we are expressing ourselves from the heart. The problem is that even the most impressively devout-sounding prayer, praise or worship might easily be nothing much more than a religious pattern.

Take prayer, for instance.

Two or three times a year I speak at dinners organized by a very energetic and effective body whose members are committed to outreach all over the world. I always enjoy these occasions, but I have noticed that a certain style of prayer seems to be mandatory for organizers and speaker before the evening gets going.

We stand in a tight circle with our arms round each other, like a small, introspective rugby scrum, bouncing on our heels (why?), shouting aggressive prayers towards the bottom of the well that is formed by our bodies. Eventually, someone will say something that sounds very much like: "One hundred and eighty!!"

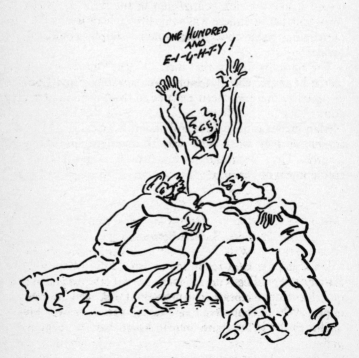

Then we get on with the meal.

There's nothing wrong with this kind of prayer – who am I to criticize, anyway? It's just that habit can breed hollowness.

I couldn't help wondering what would happen if one of these violent-prayer merchants took over a greengrocer's shop, and, at the same time, happened to have no outlet for his religious fervour.

It might be a bit like this.

Cabbages

Scene: A Greengrocer's, Shopkeeper, Customer and a pile of cabbages,

SHOPKEEPER: Good morning, madam. How may I help you?

CUSTOMER: I'd like a nice cabbage, please.

SHOPKEEPER: A nice cabbage?

CUSTOMER: Yes, please (*indicating*). That one will do nicely, thank you.

SHOPKEEPER: Just one moment, sister. That one will *not* do nicely.

CUSTOMER: It won't? Well, how about – ?

SHOPKEEPER: I think we should seek the will of God here. Do you witness to that, sister?

CUSTOMER: Well, I just want a cabbage really. I'm not sure –

SHOPKEEPER: Let's take it to the Lord. Let's just take it to him. (*Starts to pray*). Lord, we know that you chose a cabbage for our sister here before the world began, and we pray for your guidance now. We know that the world sees the outside of these cabbages, but, Lord, you see the inside. You see the heart. We pray that our sister's cabbage will have a heart for you, Lord.

We *claim* this cabbage! We *seal* this cabbage! Take dominion over your greens, Lord!

Lord, we ask that, like these fruits of thy bounty, we shall happily be sliced, boiled, drained and consumed for you, Lord. Bless your chosen cabbage to our sister, Lord, and our Sister to her rightful cabbage. Whether it be a companion to the sausage, Lord. Or, Lord, a neighbour to the fish-finger. Or peradventure Lord, an accessory to the veal cutlet: they and we are but cole-slaw in your hands, and we just ask now that we shall make a decision according to your will.

Lord, we know that in your eyes there is no such thing as a Methodist cabbage, or a Pentecostal sprout, or a Strict and Particular turnip, or a Quaker carrot, or a United Reformed aubergine, or a Salvation Army swede, or a Baptist leek, or a Anglican potato. Lord, we're all just vegetables in your sight. And now we pray for your guidance on our sister's behalf.

And we say to the caterpillars of doubt and the slugs of uncertainty – we say "Go! Right now! We rebuke you and we dismiss you and we cast you out from among these cabbages – right now!"

And now, Lord, we ask that your servant's appointed cabbage will just *rise up*! (*One cabbage springs into the air and is caught by the shopkeeper who drops it*

*casually into a bag and hands it to the
customer)* That'll be seventy-five pence,
please.

CUSTOMER: Thank you! 'Morning! (*Exit*)

END

Doors

The language of the Bible and the Church (and the world, for that matter) is full of richness. Why, then, do so many choose to live in poverty? Are we frightened of language? Do we fear a serious distribution problem when, after taking all we need, we are left with twelve gloriously, extravagantly superfluous baskets of delicious, assorted words?

Take metaphor, for instance. We've only got about two. Here's one of them that may well have passed its sell-by date.

Doors

INTERVIEWER: Now, Mr Williams, you and your wife have a recent experience of seeking guidance. Tell us about it, will you?

WILLIAMS: Well, what happened was – we tried one door that we thought the Lord was opening for us, but when, as it were, we pushed it, we found that it was shut. So we tried another door and this time it did open, so we passed through, and on the other side there was another door, but this one was shut like the first door. And when we turned round and tried to go back through the previous door – that is, the second door – we discovered that it had shut behind us, so we were in fact trapped between the two doors, so we had to climb out, as it were, through the

skylight, and we came down through another skylight and found ourselves in front of, err . . . a fourth door. This door was slightly ajar so I pushed it, but it was on a very strong spring, and it swung back and hit me quite hard on the face. So I did rebuke the door – and all the other doors, actually – at that stage, and we did wonder whether doorways might create openings through which something demonic can come. So we decided

then to seek the Lord's will by laying a
fleece, but . . . well, the Lord shut that
door.

INTERVIEWER: Mr Williams, what exactly were you and
your wife seeking guidance over?

WILLIAMS: Whether to have an open-plan house or
not . . .

Allegory

I am a great admirer of C. S. Lewis's Narnia books. Quite
apart from pure entertainment value, they open up all sorts
of ideas and perspectives that are interesting to juggle with.
Most children love them, whatever some sniffy people
may say, and you don't need to know anything about
Christianity to enjoy them.

What about modern so-called "Christian Books" for
children? There are some good ones, of course, but I find
the punch-in-the-mouth metaphors employed in some
publications quite repellent, and I don't know what the
point of such shallow writing could possibly be.

I could ramble on in this vein for page after page, but
I've already written on the subject in one or two other
books, and you're probably asking yourself how I can
criticize other people for being shallow when I don't mind
being boring.

All right! I give in – here is my own "Allegory".

Allegory

"Where on earth is Flossy-Anne?"

Pimply's voice floated into the drawing-room from the patio outside the open French windows. Sticky and Fangio looked up from the sea of home-made bread, fresh eggs, boiled ham, farmhouse butter, thick strawberry jam, rich plum cake and creamy cow's milk that Auntie Enid made them plough through every time they came home for the hols.

Sticky was a sturdy twelve-year-old with an open, frank expression under fair sticking-up hair. Auntie Enid had called him Sticky since he was a little boy, not just because of his hair, but also because of a certain moistness in his handshake.

"I haven't seen Flossy-Anne for ages", muttered Fangio. "Sisters are nothing but a nuisance, aren't they, Sticky?"

The two friends grinned at each other. Sticky loathed eleven-year-old Pimply just as much as Fangio detested ten-year-old Flossy-Anne. Fangio was a dark, moody boy capable of manly impulses, but only very infrequently.

"I think she's still up in Auntie Enid's wardrobe", called Sticky through a mouthful of half-masticated farmhouse butter.

"Oh, no, she's not looking for secret worlds again, is she?" Pimply's voice conveyed a mixture of exasperation and fondness as she ducked into the room. Well over six feet tall, Pimply had been given her nickname by Auntie Enid to take attention away from her height, but as her complexion deteriorated so she had seemed to "grow into her name", as Auntie Enid put it.

"Well, what if I was? We haven't had a decent allegory for ages."

The high, lisping voice coming from the doorway that

led into the hall announced that the fourth member of the party was present. Fangio's younger sister, Flossy-Anne, was a fluffy-haired little girl with bulging eyes and a permanent expression of surprise on her face. One of her arms was slightly longer than the other.

"So there you all are!" The voice was muffled.

All eyes swivelled upwards towards the skylight, as Auntie Enid's face appeared behind the glass. Swinging the window open she dropped a rope-end into the room and was soon lowering her bikini-clad figure to the floor.

"I want a word with you lot!" she said. "I've been trying to relax on the roof, and all I can hear is crashing noises. What's going on?"

Flossy-Anne turned bright purple and tried unsuccessfully to hide a small axe behind her back. The other children grinned at each other. Flossy-Anne always seemed to select the wrong arm!

"I'm afraid that was me," she said. "I was knocking out the back of your wardrobe, looking for Narnia. It wasn't there", she added, looking so half-witted that even Auntie Enid had to laugh.

"You children and your allegories", she smiled. "Can't we have just one school holiday when you do something a bit less symbolic?"

Auntie Enid looked at her four charges with a mixture of fondness and exasperation. They all grinned at each other. Sticky, Pimply, Fangio and Flossy-Anne had been spending their school hols with Auntie Enid for the last twenty-four years. None of them ever grew any older, and they had never yet been known to use a lavatory.

"Look at what happened yesterday," said Auntie Enid, "Sticky tried to get into the picture on his bedroom wall, didn't you, Sticky?"

Sticky grinned.

"And the day before that I had to call the fire brigade to rescue Fangio from the bottom of that old hollow oak tree at the bottom of the garden."

Fangio looked at her with a mixture of fondness and exasperation.

"It's all very well for you, Auntie Enid," he said, "you're an adult Christian. Life is one long spiritual adventure for you. We kids have difficulty understanding that. We need to experience reality through synchronistic fantasy. Besides, after twenty-four years we're allegory junkies. We need our fix, and that's why we're all hunting for this summer's secret entrance. I'm going to have a look down the lavatory bowl tomorrow — after all, it's quite hygenic because we never use it."

Auntie Enid sighed. "Well, I don't know what to say. I've grinned, and I've looked at you with a mixture of fondness and exasperation. What more can I do?"

"Well, I think Auntie Enid's right", said Pimply earnestly. "Why can't we stay here and go to church and have real adventures with God like the grown-ups do?"

Although Fangio detested his sister he was very fond of her as well. He hated to see her make a fool of herself.

"Pimply", he said kindly, "it's got to be allegory because allegory sells where spiritual adventure won't. Think secular, think W. H. Smith, think Waterstone's, think Dillons. If nobody reads us we don't exist, right?"

"I'll check the cellar for secret doors tomorrow", said Pimply.

They all grinned at each other.

Playing Games

Our writer now seems to have been resurrected. He's back on earth and getting a bit worried about his royalties — if there are any.

In every area of specifically Christian work the tension

between commercial and spiritual considerations can produce all sorts of games that have to be played out appropriately before a resolution can be reached.

I do hope old Rodney gets what he really needs.

Playing Games

W = WRITER
P = PUBLISHER

W: Hello, Crystal, it's Rodney here – Rodney Fuller.

P: Rodney! Great! How *are* you? Great to hear your voice!

W: I'm fine, Crystal. I was just ringing to ask how the book's going.

P: The book! Well –

W: Yes, my children's allegory – *Slubglab's Splod*.

P: Ah, right! Well, Rodney, we feel tremendously encouraged!

W: You do? By the sales, you mean?

P: We regard your book as a very significant addition to our back-list.

W: Oh! But in terms of sales – I wondered – I mean – things are a bit tight. I wondered if there are going to be royalties coming up when –

P: Rodney, we're all of us – publishers and writers – part of the Lord's team in this, aren't we? That's my priority, anyway.

W: Mmm . . . it's just that you don't seem to have put much into publicity, really.

P: You have to bear in mind that publishing is a commercial operation, Rodney. We can't afford to be airy-fairy, can we? Publicity is expensive.

W: Well, how many copies have actually been sold?

P: We're tremendously encouraged!

W: Yes, you said that before, but you still haven't told me the actual figures.

P: Okay, let me put it like this – the moment we hit the five thousand mark we'll be reprinting immediately – or sooner!

W: I've sold nearly five thousand then?

P: Well, no, but if we ever did hit the five thousand mark we'd –

W: Crystal, how many books have I sold?

P: What do we get from tiny acorns, Rodney?

W: Mighty oaks! How many books have I sold?

P: How many people did Our Lord use as a basis for the world-wide Church?

W: Twelve! How many books – wait a minute! Are you saying that I've sold *twelve* copies! Twelve! You told me that this book was going to change the face of children's literature in the twentieth century! How's it going to do that if only twelve people have bought it?

P: Of course I didn't mean that, Rodney. We have had a little problem – err . . . just after your book came out we found there was already a children's book on the market called *Slodglub's Slab*, which is not unlike *Slubglab's Splod*, so that did create a titchy-witchy problem. But, no, your sales are well up in the high, err . . . well, err . . . well, well, we're tremendously encouraged.

W: I'm fed up with this, Crystal! I might as well tell you – I've got myself an agent.

P: You've what? An agent? Rodney, this is terrible! This is – wait a minute. Is he a Christian?

W: Yes, he is.

P: Ah, that's all right then . . .

END

Trapeze

When I first started writing I was advised to "study the market". This is very good advice, especially for anyone who wants to write for a particular type of magazine or journal. I bought all the Christian magazines and newspapers and looked through them to see what sort of thing I should be producing.

As far as I could see, the most popular type of article was one in which someone who had just written a book lectured his or her readers, gently but firmly, on the subject of their failure to perform satisfactorily in some crucial area of their lives. The article would be accompanied by a box containing five, eight or even ten handy points to remind readers how it should be done. I tried to write such an article myself, but I didn't feel very comfortable about it.

It was only Andy Butcher's inventiveness and Mary Reid's courage that enabled something as unusual as the *Sacred Diary!* to appear, as it originally did, in column form in *Family Magazine*.

My advice to a new writer nowadays would be very similar to that which I received, except that I would add something. Once you have studied the market and thoroughly understood it – do something different. Do something that reflects what, where and who you are. Find out who created whatever boundaries you come across and, if it wasn't God, look at them very carefully indeed.

I very much enjoyed writing the piece that follows, but I do hope the style and content that I am caricaturing will go the way of the dinosaurs before too long. If you want an example of Chrisitan literature with a real edge – try the Bible.

Trapeze

Trembling with fear, the elderly lady gripped the trapeze bar so tightly that her knuckles whitened under the pressure. Glancing down at the sawdust floor a hundred feet below the tiny platform on which she balanced, she silently asked herself yet again, why, at the age of eighty-three, she was about to leap into space, supported only by the slender length of wood that her arthritic hands were clutching with such nervous intensity. Moistening dry lips with the tip of her tongue she tried hard to remember the advice that Dave and Sheena had given her.

"Don't look down – concentrate on what's happening up here. Remember that God created gravity as well as everything else . . ."

Suddenly it was time to go. Gently but firmly, Dave's hands pressed into the small of her back until she toppled over the edge of the platform and found herself swinging out and across the open space beneath the canvas ceiling of the huge tent. There was a moment's exhilaration followed by a stab of fear as she felt the bar sliding slowly but inexorably from her grasp. Dimly she was aware of Sheena's encouraging smile as the opposite trapeze swung past, and then she was falling down and down until, with a bone-shuddering jar her body hit the safety-net, bounced two or three times, then came to rest like a pound of sausages in a string-bag. A few bruises, a minor fracture here and there perhaps, but, as the octogenarian acrobat was lifted carefully from the net, there was a smile on her face. A faint cry of "Hallelujah!" from the platform high above indicated Dave's awareness that he and Sheena had yet another satisfied "customer"!

It is ten years since Dave Bolden, now a slim and well-preserved man in his early forties, first realized that God was telling him, in no uncertain terms, that acrobatics on the high trapeze are for the whole Church, not just for a specially selected few.

"I fought against it for a while," says Dave, his handsome face breaking into a grin as he remembers, "but after a couple of falls from a hundred feet without a safety net I began to think very seriously about the direction I was going in. The Lord has such a sense of humour!" he chuckles.

What about scriptural support for these revelations?

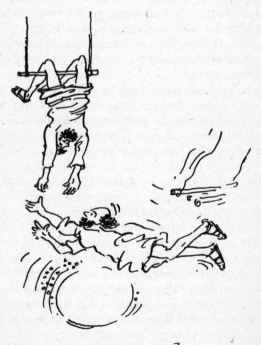

WHAT WAS THAT ABOUT GENTILES, PETE?

"Let's face it," avers Dave wryly, "you can prove or disprove just about anything you like if you don't mind twisting Bible verses to make them fit the truth as you want to see it. I have to say, though, that my own reading of Acts in particular suggests that, possibly Peter, and certainly Paul the apostle, were very fine performers on the flying trapeze in their own right. In fact, it seems clear to me that aerial acrobatics was a normal and acceptable part of day-to-day life in the early Church. It's fallen into disuse in this age and we just want to do something about it."

Did Dave encounter any special problems in setting up his ministry?

An awe-struck expression appears on Dave's well-chiselled features. "It was a real miracle, especially when it came to getting a big-top." He shakes his head in disbelief. "I was literally led step by step. I bought a magazine called *Big Tops for Sale* – quite by chance, you understand – and I was flicking idly through it one day, when an advert seemed to leap off the page, and hit me between the eyes. It said 'Big Top for sale' and there was a telephone number."

Dave's attractive and expertly made-up wife, Sheena, takes up the story, her green eyes shining with excitement.

"I dialled the number and when I spoke to the man at the other end I could hardly believe my ears. He had a big top for sale! The amount of money he wanted was almost exactly the amount of money that we had to spend."

Dave picks up the thread.

"We weren't quite sure what to do then, so we rang around our Christian friends for advice." Tears well up in Dave's eyes as he continues. "It was amazing! They *all* said the same thing. Why not suggest to the man that we give him the amount of money he wants and he gives us his big top in exchange? When we rang him back and put this to him he agreed on the spot, and that seemed like a sort of final confirmation. We were so excited that Sheena leaped up on to my shoulders and did a double backward somersault with pike and triple twist into my paternal grandfather who was staying at the time."

Sheena giggles, showing two rows of perfectly formed teeth.

"I did get a little excited," she confesses with a mischievous twinkle, "but grandpops understood – once he regained consciousness."

They laugh and look into each other's eyes. This couple are still very much in love.

Over the course of the last decade many folk have "swung for God" as Dave pursues his deeply held conviction that the Lord would have all his people involved in high trapeze work. Have some sections of the Church been less ready to respond than others?

Dave nods seriously. "The elderly infirm have been very sluggish in their response, so too have partially-sighted and blind folk. They are particularly reluctant to step off the platform once we get them up there." His normally cheerful face clouds over suddenly. "I guess it's a matter of trust. The world says it makes no sense to step into space a hundred feet above the ground when you're blind and have no experience of trapeze work, but we are not of the world and ought to be different really."

Are there dangers?

The old smile returns to Dave's face. He catches Sheena's eye and they both laugh. They've been asked this question many times in the past.

"Let me put it like this", he explains, "it's far less dangerous than strolling across the M25 with a blindfold on when the traffic is moving at maximum speed. Why do anything as risky as that when you could be here doing something really worthwhile?"

The question seems unanswerable and, in any case, there is no time for a reply. In the distance two men can be seen stretchering in the next candidate for high-flying obedience. With a flashing smile from Sheena, and a friendly wave from Dave, the trim couple are gone. Christians are often told that it's a good thing to keep their "feet on the ground". People who know Dave and Sheena Bolden are not quite so sure!

Dave Bolden's Five Helpful Hints

1) **DO** contact your nearest circus and ask how accessible they are prepared to be to church members. Christians have a God-given right to the use of trapeze equipment.

2) **DON'T** be afraid to insure your life before "taking the plunge". Christians are not called upon to abandon commonsense just because they're doing what God has told them to do!

3) **DO** speak to your vicar, elder, or church leader about wanting to perform acrobatics a hundred feet above the ground. He will certainly have some helpful things to say.

4) **DON'T** be put off by "horror stories" spread by others. People who talk about death and serious injury are very rarely the ones who have actually suffered such things.

5) **DO** remember that non-believing circus employees will be watching as you ascend to that little platform. If you're up there with a long face, and "I FEEL TENSE" written all over you, what are they going to make of the Christian faith? Enjoy yourself – and let it show!

Starting a Meeting

I have included the following piece at the last moment because it was inspired by a sermon that I heard just the other day. If you can imagine Basil Fawlty, converted but not changed, making his convoluted way through the business of starting a meeting in a very "unadorned" church, then you will easily picture the chap who is delivering this "message".

I would have included the rest of his talk, but a book can only be so long, and I fear your head would spin off and go into orbit. It might anyway.

Starting a Meeting

Can I start by suggesting that if I come back *now* to something I shall have said earlier, it will save a great deal of time in a minute? Is that clear?

I'm going to begin by telling a humorous story. The purpose of this is to relax you, the congregation, so that you will be more receptive to the serious points that I shall subsequently make. So, if you are taking notes I would suggest that you refrain from recording any of the first section because it will *be* the humorous story. Do, however, feel free to record the humorous story if you would like to pass it on to somebody else after the service, though naturally there will be no point in passing on the humorous story to anyone who is present now because, of course, they will have already heard it, unless, that is, they have to leave in the middle of the humorous story, before its climactic peak has been reached.

After the humorous story is concluded, and the laughter

thus engendered has died away, I shall speak under three headings, each beginning with a "P". Plague, Punishment and Pestilence – three areas which, I believe, beautifully illustrate the love of God.

But first, as promised, the relaxing humorous story. Those of you who are feeling tense this morning will, in a minute or so, be relaxed enough to hear scriptural judgement pronounced upon those of us for whom it is intended.

This humorous story is one which, in its original form, is quite unsuitable for the elect. I have therefore adapted the content so that it is no less humorous, but considerably more edifying.

It concerns a male person who questions another male person in the following fashion.

"Who was that lady I saw you with last night?"

The other male person replies in tones of righteous, but quite justifiable, indignation, with these words.

"The lady in question happens to be my marital partner, and has been so for some three decades."

I shall wait a few moments now while the laughter provoked by the humorous story runs its course. Settle down please.

Well, that is the end of the fun section and now I feel sure that most of us are more than ready for our first "P" of the morning.

Plague! And how we do need it in the Church today . . .

Images of God

The worship of false images is not a sin that tends to be discussed very much in the twentieth-century Church. When it *is* mentioned it's usually equated with excessive attachment to possessions, such as cars or houses. After all, you don't see too many golden calves or images of Baal in your average British sitting-room.

There is, however, another, and more subtly destructive way in which this commandment continues to be disobeyed – by Christians.

We all do it to a lesser or greater extent. Because of individual upbringing, life experiences and inherited patterns of response, we tend to invest our personal images of God with attributes that have more to do with us than with God as he actually is.

Often, and perhaps more commonly, people have difficulty in separating the concept of God as father, from memories of their own unsatisfactory parent. Earthly fathers can be cruel or over-indulgent or emotionally chaotic. The child in us clings unconsciously to these negative recollections, unable to allow the idea of God as a perfect father to sink successfully from head to heart.

Within any one congregation a strange and varied selection of God-images will be prayed to and worshipped each Sunday.

I have recorded elsewhere how a friend of mine on hearing Bishop Peter Ball talk about his faith, said, "He knows a different God to the one I do – his God's nice!"

There are many distorted views of the divine personality. Here are three of the most common ones.

Images of God

1) **God as bank manager.**

> Ah, Mr Brown, do please sit down,
> Now what are we to do?
> For, once, you banked with us, but now,
> We seem to bank with you.

Your sin account is overdrawn,
With lust and sloth and pride,
And, dear, dear, dear, there's little here,
Upon the credit side.
Against the veritable sea,
Of evil you have done,
There's one small act of kindness,
Back in nineteen-sixty-one.
In fact your banking record,
From the moment you were born,
Is such that we may well decide,
Your Access is withdrawn.

2) God as a senile old man

Hello! Yes, this is God – speak up!
Hello! What's that you say?
Well, if you say you did, you did,
I didn't hear you pray.
You say you asked me several times?
Well, nowadays I find,
That even quite important things
Just seem to slip my mind.
Oh, yes, that is a problem,
But there's little I can do,
My angels are quite elderly,
They've all got fowlpest too.
I wouldn't bother being good,
You'll only end up bored,
It's not exactly heaven,
In a geriatric ward.

3) God as a hippy

Nothing's wrong and nothing's right,
And nothing's in between,

All this "Heh, you broke the rules",
Has never been my scene.
People go for different things.
Like Mecca and Nirvana,
Some find me in worry beads,
Or hash, or a banana.
Don't let people steer you wrong,
It's cool to sin and doubt,
Whatever gives you groovy vibes,
Just let it all hang out.
Heaven's what you make it, man,
Freedom gives you power,
Love and peace and jelly-beans,
No hassle – have a flower.

Connections to Paradise

People often ask me where writers get their ideas from. The answer, of course, is – British Rail. No, I'm only joking, although, when you travel by train as much as I do, you do hear some wonderful things. Take the other day, for instance. I was sitting on a train, in a fairly crowded compartment, when the guard's voice came over the loudspeaker system. It began in that flatly repetitive tone beloved of guards everywhere, but it quite quickly turned into a strangled bleat.

"Like to advise customers that the next station stop will be Darnley Halt. (*Pause*) Darnley Halt has a very short platform. (*Longer pause*) Customers wishing to alight at Darnley Halt should move to the front of the train. The front of the train (*Worried pause*) is situated (*Very worried pause*) at the end (*Pause indicative of realization that there is no way out of sentence with honour*) farthest (*Pause of utter panic*) from (*Pause as guard plays wildly with *alternative endings to his sentence, such as: " . . . The Platonic Ideal", or "Patagonia") the back . . ." (Miserable silence as guard covers head with arms and vows to stay locked in little guard compartment for rest of journey)*

No, it isn't always British Rail, but it's certainly true that most of my ideas spring from relatively ordinary day-to-day incidents.

"Yes," says the questioner when I explain this, "but nothing ever happens to me – nothing worth recording in detail, anyway."

I don't think this is true. Lots of different things happen to all of us; the difference, perhaps, is that the writer makes a conscious mental (or written) note of his or her experiences and, even more importantly, goes on to forge or discover the kind of connections that add depth and significance to quite ordinary observations.

Let me give you an example.

Connections to Paradise

One morning I was travelling by train from Polegate, in Sussex, down to Southampton for a day of promotion in connection with my latest book. I knew I had to change at Brighton, but I wasn't quite sure whether the journey was straight through after that. I went into the travel-centre on Brighton station to check.

Travel-centres are strange places. They seem to be staffed by people who go off sick in packs of four. They always leave behind a nice but nervy person who will burst into tears if too much pressure is put on them. In addition, the queue in front of you invariably consists of a ninety-year-old Ukranian who speaks no English, weeps passionately but inexplicably at regular intervals, and needs to get to Clitheroe via Taunton on a sleeper in six weeks' time, and a very, very lonely person who always comes down there on that day, at that time, to while away an hour or so with the nice, nervy person who doesn't mind because it never involves any nasty, awkward questions about train times.

Thank goodness Brighton travel-centre is nothing like that. I had no trouble at all.

"Change at Hove, sir," trilled the young girl behind the counter, "you'll pick up a Southampton train there."

"Thank you!" I called over my shoulder as I went back out to the station concourse.

On my way to the appropriate platform I glanced up at the electronic information board, just hoping for a little comfortable confirmation. No such luck!

"*Passengers for Southampton should change at Worthing*", announced the board in large white letters.

Somewhat dismayed, I stopped at the ticket barrier and spoke to the bored young man who was slumped on a stool inside his little shelter.

"Tell me," I said, "if you were me, where would you change for Southampton on this train?"

"Portsmouth", he replied with gloomy certainty.

"Portsmouth?" I repeated. "Are you sure?"

"Change at Portsmouth for Southampton", he said, in that wearily sarcastic manner that people reserve for those who haven't understood the first time.

Muttering thanks I hurried along the platform to board my train, and was just about to get on when I surrendered to a wild impulse to ask just once more for this surprisingly elusive piece of information. An elderly, white-haired, rather avuncular looking British Rail employee was pushing a trolley past me. This was a man to be trusted – a man who would know!

"Excuse me", I called.

The man stopped his trolley and beamed at me with fatherly kindness. "'Ow can I 'elp you, sir?" he said.

I explained that I had been offered three quite different pieces of advice and wasn't sure which one to follow. He chuckled tolerantly.

"Bless 'em, sir, they don't know nothin', these young things. If you take this train you wanna change at Havant for Southampton, sir. You'll pick one up there all right."

"Oh well," I said to myself as I settled down in the corner of a carriage at last, "at least I know now – change at Havant . . ."

A few minutes later the ticket inspector arrived. He was a youngish man with a heavy Indian accent.

"Change at Havant for Southampton, don't I?" I enquired lightly, certain that he would agree.

"You need to go upstairs, sir," he replied, "upstairs for Southampton."

I stared at him for a moment, my senses reeling. Upstairs? Upstairs for Southampton? Had I, without realizing it, boarded some kind of new double-decker train, the top half of which went to Southampton, while the bottom half didn't? How could that be . . .?

"Upstairs? " I repeated faintly, "I don't . . ."

"Upstairs at Portsmouth station," continued my informant, "upstairs to the upper platform for the train to Southampton, sir. That is what you must do."

And that piece of advice was, I'm pleased to say, absolutely correct.

That is what happened, and it is completely true.

Connections? Well, it occurred to me afterwards that my succession of advisers, all employed by the same company, and all offering diverse views on the same subject, were rather like the Christian denominations, each with its own clear idea about how people should get to the place where they are going, and each adamant that their way is the only one worth considering.

Where *do* we change for Paradise?

Precious

For years I tried to exercise ministries that I had not got. It didn't work.

I did *not* have a ministry of reconciliation. I had a ministry of making things worse, and ending up with everyone disliking me as well as each other.

I did *not* have a ministry of wisdom and special insight. I had a ministry of getting things wrong and upsetting people.

I did *not* have a ministry of prayer. I had a ministry of promising people I would pray for them, and then forgetting to do it, and getting very embarrassed when they thanked me and said that they knew my prayers had helped, and feeling guilty because I couldn't quite bring myself to tell them the truth.

I did *not* have a ministry of evangelism. I had a ministry of putting forward arguments so hopelessly ill-prepared and half-baked that I became progressively less convinced myself as I went on speaking, and ended up in a state of miserable agnosticism.

I did *not* have a ministry of prophetic absailing, although it broke my heart to have finally to face that realization.

Perhaps there are signs of a genuine ministry developing nowadays, but I'm certainly not going to put a name to what I think it might be.

Here's a ludicrously exaggerated version of what goes wrong when a "ministry of encouragement" is exercised so liberally that the encouragement becomes devalued to the point of being rather meaningless.

Precious

Leader, Stanley, George (a newcomer), Veronica and Penelope are sitting in a semi-circle. They all have open Bibles on their laps.

LEADER: Right, now, we've read the passage of scripture that tells us the story of Zacchaeus, and I'm going to ask that we might share our insights as we feel led so to do.
(*Pause*)

STANLEY: Well, I was thinking . . .

LEADER: Yes, Stanley, go ahead.

GEORGE: Yeah, go fer it, Stan!

STANLEY: Well, I was thinking that Zacchaeus was up a tree, and a tree's got leaves, right?

LEADER: Yes?

STANLEY: Yes, and God *leaves* us to deal with certain things on our own. He *leaves* us, doesn't he?

LEADER: Well, isn't that interesting? *Isn't* that interesting? Do you know – I never made that connection before. Leaves on the tree, and he *leaves* us. *Isn't* that interesting? (*Pause*) Any other insights to share?

VERONICA: I noticed that Zacchaeus begins with the last letter of the alphabet, and, when you think of it, the last thing God wants us to do is disobey him. It's the *last* thing he wants us to do, and Zacchaeus begins with the *last* letter of the alphabet.

LEADER: Isn't that special? That's *very* special. The last thing God wants is disobedience, and Zacchaeus begins with . . . that's very special – *very* special. Veronica has given us something very special, hasn't she, everybody?
(*All nod except George, who shakes his head in puzzlement*)

PENELOPE: May I share?

LEADER: Please do, Penelope. Mmmm!

PENELOPE: I feel that this passage is really about serving. Zacchaeus was asked to serve – not just serve the food, but to serve the Lord. We should all serve. He's called us to serve, and when we do serve we in our turn will be served. Not just serving because we're told to serve, but serving with joy because we want to serve the one who served us.

LEADER: Isn't that precious? What a precious thing to share. We're called to serve – we're all called to serve each other. What a new and precious thought. Bless you, Penelope, for that very precious gift to us. (*Pause*) George, you're new here, but have you any err . . .

GEORGE: Well, I'm not sure I've got the 'ang of this, but I was thinkin' that once old Zack was –

LEADER: Zacchaeus.

GEORGE: Once old Zacchaeus was – like – back on the ground . . .

LEADER: Yes?

GEORGE: Well, everyone must've realized 'e was a scone short of a cream tea, mustn't they?

LEADER: A scone short of . . .? Do you mean that he was mentally deranged?

GEORGE: Yeah, that's right, yeah.

LEADER: And why must everyone have realized that?

GEORGE: Well, s'obvious, innit? Because . . . (*Pause*) 'e was out of 'is tree! Out of 'is tree – gettit? 'E was out of 'is tree!
(*Laughs raucously*)

LEADER: (*When George has finished laughing*) Well, isn't that silly. That's *very* silly. That was a silly thing to share, wasn't it, everybody?

GEORGE: Why? 'Ow come 'is was interestin', an' 'ers was special, an 'ers was precious, but mine's silly? Anyway, Precious laughed, didn't you Precious? Old Special looked a bit upset, but Precious was well away, weren't you, Precious? Couldn't 'elp it, could yer?

PENELOPE: (*No longer laughing*) If you call me Precious one more time I shall break my chair over your head!

GEORGE: Well, that's special, innit? That's interestin'. That's a very precious gift to me, innit? Breakin' a chair over me 'ead! (*To Penelope*) Thank you for offering to share your chair with me. What d'yer make of that, chief? I bet old Zacchaeus wouldn't 'ave done that once 'e got Jesus 'ome an' sat down at the table – crept up behind 'im an' broken a chair over 'is 'ead. I bet –

STANLEY: May I share an urge?
(*Pause*)

GEORGE: (*Warily*) That's interestin', innit?

STANLEY: I'd like to suggest that we forgive our brother

George fully and freely, just as Zacchaeus was forgiven for all his past offences.

LEADER: Well, isn't that lovely. *Isn't* that lovely! Isn't that a lovely unselfish thought, everybody?

GEORGE: Yeah, that's lovely all right. Only reason I'm 'ere is 'cos old Stan 'adn't got a lift tonight, an' 'e knows 'e won't get 'ome unless 'e does a grease-job on yours truly. That's a lovely unselfish thought, Stan, old mate. That's —

LEADER: Just a minute. Did you really give Stanley a lift here tonight, George? Did you do that for him?

GEORGE: Well . . . yeah, I did.

LEADER: Well, isn't that . . . That's really . . . (*Searches for appropriate word*)

PENELOPE: Surprising?

LEADER: Now, now, Precious — I mean — Penelope, there is something very beautiful about George bringing Stanley here in his car without any thought of personal cost. Isn't that beautiful, everybody?

STANLEY: He charged me the same as a taxi would have done — Sunday rate. That's double.

LEADER: Oh! Well, that's not quite so beautiful, is it?

GEORGE: Ah, well I *'ad* to charge 'im, see?

LEADER: You had to?

GEORGE: Yeah! I needed the money for the same reason that old Zacchaeus 'ad to climb the tree.

LEADER: And that reason was . . .?

GEORGE: Well, like old Zacchaeus . . .

LEADER: Yes?

GEORGE: I was a bit short. Gettit? A bit short! (*Laughs*)

LEADER: Let's close by joining together in a physical attack on George. Won't that be lovely?

STANLEY: That's a very interesting prospect.

VERONICA: Very special.
PENELOPE: Precious!
(*They converge on him*)

END

Gig-Along-A-God

Our writer has now had a stroke of really bad luck. The poor fellow has been renamed Cedric Spamrumbler (as if he hadn't got enough problems already). He is about to come face to face with the "famous Christian" machine, that strange mechanism that takes very ordinary people and turns them into *well-known* very ordinary people.

The significant point, of course, is that dear old Cedric is very anxious to meet his hypothetical public halfway. Once he's established he'll be free to say that fame and popularity were never motivating forces in his "ministry".

Oh, Cedric!

Gig-Along-A-God

W = WRITER
A = AGENT

W: Good morning – err . . . is this the agency?
A: Yes, indeed, sir, we are the "Gig-along-a-God Christian Performance Agency: Charismatics for Conferences, Prophets for Parties, Evangelicals for Events, Bible-scholars for Beanos, Mystics for Mainstage, Marquees and Marriages, Healers for Hoe-downs, Parsons for Picnics and Theologians for Theatricals: Bless-O-

Grams a speciality: all prices include VAT and will be
tithed at source." Is your social engagement heading
for disaster? My name is Grace. How may I serve you?

W: Well, err . . . I want to be a cult.

A: You want to be . . . ?

W: I want to be on the fringe at Green Harvest and
Springbelt. I want to be famous! I want to be
recognized! I want some respect! I want to be a star!!
(*Pause*) for the Lord . . .

A: Our brochure does guarantee humility in *all* performers, Mister err . . .

W: Spamrumbler – Cedric Spamrumbler

A: Well, that would certainly keep *me* humble. So, Mister
Spamrumbler – what is your normal occupation?

W: Well, I'm a Christian writer – it's a very lonely job
y'know. I thought maybe a bit of public exposure
might make life a bit brighter and push the sales a bit
and – (*Suddenly crazed*) I wanna sign autograph
books! I want to be endearingly self-effacing when I'm
interviewed in front of hundreds of people! I want –

A: Mister Spamrumbler, what was the title of your last
book?

W: It was called *An exegetical analysis of philosophical
infrastructures in post-alluvial didacticism* – Volume
nine.

A: Hmmm . . . not the sort of thing you can turn into a
musical, is it? Are there any funny bits in it?

W: There are some references to mythical incongruity in
the context of evolutionary antitheses that certainly
make me chuckle.

A: Mmm, yes, what a hoot . . . I'm not sure we're quite
getting there yet, Mister Spamrumbler. What about
something juicy in the past that you've had a wonderful deliverance from? That always goes down very
well. Ever been on drugs? Drink? Contact with the
occult? Been in prison? Ever been involved with some
big scandal in the papers – "Playboy Peer Slams Neo-

nazi Darby and Joan Club" – that sort of thing?

W: The only thing I can remember (*Glances guiltily round*) well – last year I slightly over-filled my salad bowl during a visit to my local Pizza Land restaurant. I don't know why I did it. I – I just lost my head!

A: Mmm, yes, I think we can do something with that. "Greed Leads Top Christian Academic to Defraud Huge Food Chain". I'll get that in the Christian press for the month after next. Tomorrow morning I'll get on to a contact at the publisher's and have a contract drawn up for – let's say – a 40,000 word paperback, thousand pound advance. Title – let's see; something like: "From Gluttony to God – one man's journey from the gutter of slavering, greed and lust to the peace of personal renewal". Be out by next spring – and we should have you doing seminars on Dieting, Gluttony, Anorexia, Cookery, Significance of bread in the New Testament, and Occult influence on the pizza – by, well, by autumn at the earliest. How does that sound, Mister Spamrumbler?

W: Well, it sounds fine! What about money? How much will I have to pay you?

A: It's customary to pay a percentage to the agent, Mister Spamrumbler.

W: I see. Well, do you think we ought to pray about what the percentage should be?

A: Err . . . yes, all right. Let's err . . . pray that we will be told the appropriate figure.
(*They both pray*)

W: Ten per cent!

A: (*Almost simultaneously*) Fifteen per cent! Mmm, let's give it a few more seconds . . .
(*They pray*)

W & A: (*Simultaneously*) Twelve and a half per cent!
(*They stand and shake hands*)

END

Anglican Rap

When I told my children I was contemplating the writing of a "Rap" they were far from impressed. I think they had visions of me performing some sonorous piece of badly scanning verse whose aim was to show the youth of today that the Church is relevant to their culture. They needn't have worried. I have a deep and abiding dislike of arranged marriages between two concepts that repel each other on sight.

We have enough things in the Christian faith that are authentically and uniquely ours, without having to caper foolishly to the world's tune. Don't misunderstand me – I'm all for minimum silliness and proper cultural integration. It's the Saatchi and Saatchi approach that puts me off. Why construct a false presentation of something that's true anyway? Much better, surely, to strip away the man-made nonsense that has obscured the truth, a truth that always *was* relevant. I would rather go to a properly conducted bar, selling all the normal alcoholic drinks, and run by Christians, than crouch over my vimto in a so-called "Christian bar". But, of course, I may be quite wrong in taking that view, and how fortunate I am that those of you who *do* disagree with me will freely forgive me for my error.

The Anglican Rap is a light-hearted look at what might result from my own church's attempt to preserve itself in its most turgid form by using a "modern" device.

Anglican Rap

Let's kneel, let's stand,
Let's be terribly bland,
Let's sing quite loud with a dignified clap,
Let's process around the church in a victory lap.
Check us on the old denominational map,
From the Isle of Wight to the Watford Gap,
Everybody's doing it – the Anglican rap.
Come along and boogie to the Anglican beat,
Just grab your hermeneutics and exegete!

Take a cruise to the pews, have a snooze, read the news,
Don't go looking for disaster with a pentecostal pastor,
There'll be tongues and revelations with bizarre
    interpretations.
Don't smile when life's vile in the house-church style,
Or linger with the lost under old Rob Frost.
Do you fancy looking barmy with the silly Sally Army?
Don't meet above the baker's with the Shakers and the
    Quakers,
Or shiver in the water like the Baptists say you oughter,
We don't baptize in the bottom of a tank,
Our font is Norman, and our vicar is Frank.
We're well aware of modern theological trends,
But Frank and Norman are still good friends.
We're modern and we're modish, have you seen our
    groovy cassocks?
And we're open to the option of inflated rubber hassocks.
Be a real cool cat, be an Anglican dude,
Every now and then we're *almost* rude.

Let's kneel, let's stand,
Let's be terribly bland.

Let's sing quite loud with a dignified clap,
Let's process around the church in a victory lap.
Check us on the old denominational map,
From the Isle of Wight to the Watford Gap,
Everybody's doing it – the Anglican Rap.
Come along and boogie to the Anglican beat,
Just grab your hermeneutics and exegete.

Don't falter at the altar, have a rave in the nave,
Have a smile in the aisle, have a lapse in the apse,

Have a thriller by the pillar, eat an apple in the chapel,
Have some oysters in the cloisters, read some Auden to the
    warden,
Climb the font if you want, feel the power up the tower,
Light a torch in the porch, start a fire in the choir,
Raise your arms in the psalms, mind the gorgon at the
    organ,
Swap your knickers for the vicar's, check you're zipped in
    the crypt.
Some of us speak through tightly clenched teeth,
And lots of us look like Edward Heath. (And that's just the
    ladies)
Anglicans hurry to the old God-shack,
To be first in the queue for the seats at the back.
We're a very broad church, we're home from home,
You can chat up the vicar, or flirt with Rome.
The leader of our gang is big and scary,
He's no spring-chicken, but his name is Carey.

Let's kneel, let's stand,
Let's be terribly bland,
Let's sing quite loud with a dignified clap,
Let's process around the church in a victory lap.
Check us on the old denominational map,
From the Isle of Wight to the Watford Gap,
Everybody's doing it – the Anglican rap.
Come along and boogie to the Anglican beat,
Just grab your hermeneutics and exegete!

Dear Craig

A friend of mine who happens to be gay and a Christian
went through hell in his early attempts to find counselling
and constructive assistance from various sections of the

Church. Elementary formulae and simplistic ideas were not just unhelpful – they were sometimes terrifying. Now, thank God, he has found people and places that offer hope, because they are dealing with *him*, rather than one aspect of what he is.

That is the Jesus way.

Perhaps we should think before we produce clichéd responses to very deep problems. The following letter is extremely silly but . . .

Dear Craig

Dear Craig,

First of all, let me say how much I appreciate the fact that you have trusted me with such a delicate and personal problem. I only hope I can help a little!

Craig, I'm going to say something to you now that may surprise you. I very much doubt that you really are the only person in your church who owns a trombone. Recent and quite reliable research shows that at least one in twenty-five of all British males is in possession of a brass instrument of some kind, and yours is a large congregation. I am quite sure you are not alone.

And now for a little personal testimony. This is a private letter, so you will understand that what follows is not for sharing. A few years ago, Craig, I inherited the possessions of an elderly uncle whom I had known only slightly. When I arrived at Uncle Brendon's house to look through the items that were now mine, I discovered that my uncle had himself been the covert owner of a brass instrument. For some reasons that I do not understand I was both repulsed and fascinated by the object. Throwing all moral considerations to the wind I raised the instrument to my lips (I will not mince words with you, Craig) and blew one

indulgent blast that shattered the silence of my deceased uncle's bedroom.

Guilt encased me like a diving-suit, Craig.

Later that day I arrived home, sat my wife quietly down in the kitchen, and, taking both her hands in mine, told her as gently as I could that I now had a malignant tuba.

Clarissa and I have worked through that problem as man and wife, and I think I can honestly say that it *is* under control. I shall always have my tuba, but it has not left the closet since that day.

I inherited my wind instrument, Craig, and some people claim that they cannot be acquired in any other way. You do not say in your letter anything about the origin of your brass instrument, but I am convinced in my own mind that inheritance is not the only means by which younger *and* older folk become involved in such pursuits. (I once counselled a tone-deaf pensioner who had embezzled a tenor saxophone).

Craig, let me make the most important point of all. No one can condemn you or anyone else for owning a trombone and desiring to play it, but performance would be a sin. We love the sinner, but we hate his trombone, don't we? Let's not be misled by those who have openly formed brass-bands for performance in the church. You and I will be strong, Craig, and one day the rest of the church will know just what a debt of gratitude they owe us.

Yours in mutual restraint,

Babies and Bathwater

The Protestant Church has thrown out far too many healthy babies in its panic-stricken fear of being polluted by dirty bath water. We have suffered loss and deprivation as a result.

Negative, knee-jerk responses to Mary, the mother of Jesus, have left us with an impoverished appreciation of the female elements of divinity, and an unattractively disrespectful attitude to a very special and heroic lady.

A couple of years ago I took a midnight walk over the Downs with two friends, both from a very low-church background. As we climbed those softly-curving, motherly hills beneath the moon, I expressed my view that Mary was regarded slightly neurotically by many evangelical Christians.

People will say things on the Downs at midnight that they might not say anywhere else.

"It's funny you should say that", said one of my companions, a self-employed builder. "I was working up on a roof this week with some other blokes, and they were telling jokes and saying things that I just didn't want to hear. And then, suddenly, I felt as if a woman's hands had been placed over my ears."

We walked on in silence for a moment, then my other friend spoke.

"It *is* funny you should say that. The other day, when I was leading our church meeting, I said something or other about Mary, something sarcastic, I mean, and – I don't know how to describe it – it was as if God slapped me on the wrist. That's how it felt."

We didn't discuss those experiences any further. There was no point. None of us were about to embrace Rome. We were just opening one or two doors marked "private".

Confession is another example. Terrified of being trapped in a box with a man who is trying to do God's job for him, we heedlessly sweep away the entirely scriptural business of confessing our sins to one another. Spiritual and psychological health can sometimes depend on this process.

Often, the baby that we discard grows up elsewhere in a distorted form. Healing goes and Christian Science grows. Spiritual gifts are neglected and a doctrine of "no salvation without tongues" appears.

Death, and the whole question of communication between heaven and earth, went down the theological waste-pipe a long time ago. These issues are determinedly and consistently prevented from gurgling back to the surface by those sections of the Church whose members have managed to perfect the corporate magic act of concealing fear beneath aggressive or frenetic "now-ness". Everyone does it. Last year one of the breakfast programmes spent a week discussing the problem of road accidents involving children. A huge number of kids are killed and injured every year on our roads. Everything was discussed during that week – road safety, careless driving, the evils of drink, proper car maintenance, everything you can think of, except death. Where are all those children who have died? Does it matter? How do we educate our children in an understanding of death? No one seemed to think these questions worth asking.

Spiritualism and absorption in the occult are the mutant and very unwelcome growths that tend to fill the vacuum that is created by this kind of denial in the world and the Church.

Let's hope that we can rescue some of these "babies", wash the dirty water away and examine them carefully and calmly. Perhaps, then, people like myself, who peep fearfully out from behind the blinds of fear and prejudice, will allow Jesus to shine light into dark corners and amaze us with new and deeper discoveries.

Back to the Future

A couple of years ago we took our bicycles down to Newhaven, crossed by ferry to Northern France, and spent a few enjoyable days pedalling from town to town along the river valleys. Our last day was set aside to explore the port of Dieppe before recrossing the channel that evening.

Just after lunch we entered the cool interior of a big church near the centre of the town. I lost touch with the others for a while, but after a few minutes I discovered Katy aged four staring at a life-size sculpture of Mary, the mother of Jesus, holding her son's dead body in her arms and looking into his face with an expression of real pain and loss. Katy turned and saw me.

"Daddy, why has Jesus got a hole in his side?"

Stumblingly, I explained that a Roman spear had been responsible. Katy was horrified. She studied the sculpture again.

"Daddy he's got holes in his feet. Why has he got holes in his feet?"

"Look", I pointed to a small crucifix on the wall above us. "They nailed his feet to that piece of wood called a cross, and those are the holes where the nails were."

"Nailed his feet?!"

She turned to look at the stone figures again. Her voice broke a little as she spoke.

"Daddy, he's got holes in his hands as well. They didn't nail his hands as well did they?"

Sadly, I explained. Katy moved closer to the sculpture, put her arm around Jesus, and rested her face down on his knee.

Suddenly I longed to go back to the time when I first understood that Jesus died for me and it really hurt, before I covered my faith in words and worries. I wanted to be like a child again.

But I felt like a cabbage.

> New to me
> But old in years
> When he came
> Examined tears.
> Antique love
> Regard me now
> Love so good
> Kiss my brow.
> Complete release
> Chance to start
> Eventually
> Forgive my heart.
> Now the peace
> Waits for me
> Rest in hope
> Maybe free.